NAPOLEON HILL'S
PHILOSOPHY
OF SUCCESS

NAPOLEON HILL'S
PHILOSOPHY
OF SUCCESS

THE 17 ORIGINAL
LESSONS

MEDIA

Published 2021 by Gildan Media LLC
aka G&D Media
www.GandDmedia.com

Front Cover design by David Rheinhardt of Pyrographx

Interior design by Meghan Day Healey of Story Horse, LLC

Library of Congress Cataloging-in-Publication Data is available upon request

ISBN: 978-1-7225-0308-6

10   9   8   7   6   5   4   3   2   1

Contents

Introduction

Napoleon Hill was sixty-eight years old and living happily in semi-retirement in California with his wife Annie Lou when he was induced to start a new enterprise, Napoleon Hill Associates. It began when insurance tycoon W. Clement Stone, a long time fan of Napoleon Hill's philosophy, was invited by his dentist to hear Napoleon address a dental convention in Chicago. Stone had been giving his employees at insurance giant Combined Insurance Company of America copies of Hill's best selling book *Think And Grow Rich* for years, and was thrilled to finally meet the great philosopher.

The two men were seated together at the convention, and from their lunchtime discussion emerged the idea of establishing Napoleon Hill Associates, an organization which would train people to instruct others on how to implement the seventeen principles of success Hill had discovered through over twenty years of research. This enterprise lasted from 1952 until 1962, during which time Messrs. Hill and Stone wrote a book together, *Success Through a Positive Mental Attitude*, published a magazine titled *Success Unlimited*, and traveled extensively to teach, lecture and present radio and television programs explaining the principles of success.

In the early days of Napoleon Hill Associates, Napoleon wrote a series of seventeen lectures designed to instruct its employees and representatives about each principle of success, so that they could then teach others how to use these principles. The Trustees of the Napoleon Hill Foundation, established by Napoleon and Annie Lou in 1967, knew about the existence of these lectures (Mr. Stone was Chairman of the Foundation for more than two decades until his death in 2002), but did not have them. They were only recently discovered after the 2019 death of the Foundation's then Chairman, Dr. Charles Johnson, Napoleon Hill's nephew, and are presented here for the first time since the lectures were delivered.

Each of these lectures explains in detail the meaning, importance and means of application of the success principle it discusses. The lectures also explain the interrelationship of the principles. They were intended to serve as a training manual, but I believe you will find that they are also a very understandable and impactful "how to" guide about the many ways these success principles can be used by you, the reader, to achieve the success, happiness and peace of mind you desire.

The Trustees of the Napoleon Hill Foundation are proud and happy to partner with our esteemed publisher to bring you this long lost work of the greatest self help philosopher of all time. We are confident you will enjoy and benefit from it.

—Don M. Green
CEO and Trustee, Napoleon Hill Foundation

1

Definiteness of Purpose

Definiteness of purpose is the starting point of all achievement. It is the stumbling block of ninety-eight out of every hundred persons because they never really define their goals or start toward them with definiteness of purpose.

Think it over: 98 percent of the people of the world are drifting aimlessly through life without the slightest idea of the work for which they are fitted, and with no conception whatsoever of even the need for a definite objective toward which to strive. This is one of the greatest tragedies of civilization. I hope that you will resolve that from this day forward you will not settle with life for anything short of what you want. I hope that I shall convince you that when I say you don't have to settle for anything less than what you want, I am not just using idle words. I am making that statement from my observation of thousands of people over more than fifty years.

At this point I want to discuss ideas, for although ideas are the only asset that have no fixed value, they are the beginning of all achievements. This book has been organized for the purpose of inducing a flow of ideas through your mind. It is intended to introduce you to your other self: the self that has a vision of your innate spiritual powers and will not accept or recognize failure, but will arouse your determination to go forth and claim what is rightfully yours.

Ideas form the foundation of all fortunes and the starting point of all inventions. They have mastered the air above us and the waters of the ocean around us. They have enabled us to harness and use the energy known as the ether, with which one mind may communicate with another mind by means of telepathy. There can be no evolution of any idea without a starting point in the form of definiteness of purpose. Hence this principle takes first position in the philosophy of personal achievement.

There are big ideas behind definiteness of purpose. Certain factors that enter into the subject may be classified as mental; others might be classified as economic. I am going to analyze each one of these factors so that you will have a complete and thorough understanding of them and can take full advantage of the benefits of this great principle of personal achievement. There are seven big ideas.

The first big idea is this: *the starting point of all personal achievement is the adoption of a definite major purpose and a definite plan for its attainment.* As soon as you have decided what your definite major purpose of life is, you can expect to enjoy some of its advantages. The advantages come almost automatically.

The first advantage, *definiteness of purpose* develops (a) self-reliance, (b) personal initiative, (c) imagination, (d) enthusiasm, (e) self-discipline, and (f) concentration of effort. All of these are required for material success.

The second advantage is *specialization*. Definiteness of purpose encourages you to specialize, and specialization tends toward perfection. You will become a specialist in success. Definiteness of purpose has a way of magnetizing the mind so as to attract to you the specialized knowledge for success.

The third advantage: *budgeting of time and money.* Definiteness of purpose will induce you to budget your time and your money and plan all of your day-to-day endeavors so they lead to the attainment of your definite major purpose.

The fourth advantage: definiteness of purpose *alerts the mind to opportunities.* It gives courage for action. It makes your mind more alert to recognize opportunities related to your major purpose, and it inspires the necessary courage to act upon these opportunities when they appear.

The fifth advantage: definiteness of purpose develops *the capacity to reach decisions quickly and firmly.* Successful people make decisions quickly, as soon as all the facts are available, and change them very slowly, if ever. Unsuccessful people make decisions very slowly and change them very often and very quickly.

Ponder over this statement again, copy it down on a separate piece of paper, and pin it up in some conspicuous spot, where you will see it often. It is so valuable, in fact, that if you receive no other ideas from this book, you will have received full value for your money.

The way to develop decisiveness is to start right where you are, with the very next question that you face. Make a decision. Make any decision. Any decision is better than none. Start making up your mind.

The sixth advantage: not only does definiteness of purpose develop confidence in your own integrity and character, it *attracts the favorable attention of other people and inspires their cooperation.* The man who knows where he is going and is determined to get there will always find willing helpers along the way.

The seventh advantage: definiteness of purpose prepares the mind for *faith.* The greatest of all benefits of definiteness of purpose is that it opens the way for the full exercise of the state of mind known as faith. It makes the mind positive. It frees the mind from limitations of fear, doubt, discouragement, indecision, and procrastination. Doubt usually results in alibis, excuses, or apologies for failure. Remember, success requires no explanation. Failure permits no alibis.

The eighth advantage: definiteness of purpose *provides one with a success consciousness and protects one against the influence of failure consciousness.* Your mind becomes sold on succeeding and refuses to accept the possibility of failure.

The second big idea is this: *all individual achievements are the result of a motive or combination of motives.* The nine basic motives that inspire all voluntary action are (1) the emotion of love; (2) the emotion of sex; (3) the desire for material gain; (4) the desire for self-preservation; (5) the desire for freedom of body and mind; (6) the desire for self-expression and recognition; (7) the desire for life after death; (8) the desire for revenge; and (9) the emotion of fear.

You will find that unless the major and minor purposes of your life are supported with a proper number of these motives, you are not going to be interested in carrying out those purposes to a successful conclusion. The more positive basic motives that you have urging you on, the more likely you are to get in touch with the subconscious mind and to draw the power of Infinite Intelligence.

The first motive is *love*. It is the greatest of all motives. Love is a psychic force related to the spiritual side of man. When I speak of love, I refer not merely to the physical attraction but to love in its bigger, broader sense. Love is the greatest and most powerful motive known.

There are many kinds of love. Love of self is the lowest order, for it implies selfishness. Love of truth or principle is the highest, for it is based on righteousness. There are varieties of neighborly love: that of parents for their children and children for their parents; that of friendships; that which is regardless of age, sex, or social relationship; then the love of sweethearts.

Generally speaking, there can be three different attitudes and expressions of love: (1) the labor of love. Work which you enjoy doing, which brings forth your best of creative efforts. To have a labor of love is one of the twelve great riches of life. (2) A love of truth or principle: the love of an ideal which finds expression in one's thirst for spiritual enlightenment and a continual search for further knowledge of things as they are. A person motivated by this kind of love has true humility of heart. (3) Love of a beautiful woman or a handsome man: your girlfriend or boyfriend, your sweetheart, or your wife or husband. In this type of love there are at least three basic ingredients: (a) physical attraction, (b) affectional response, and (c) intellectual and spiritual companionship. It is only natural for a person to put forth extraordinary effort and his finest talent to please the object of his affection.

The second motive is the emotion of *sex*, which is the physical complement of love. Nature carefully applies the principle of definiteness of purpose. No more ingenious plan could be conceived than the one by which nature guarantees the perpetuation of life. The desire for physical expression of the mating instinct is the most powerful of human emotions. Under this urge, individuals develop imagination, fortitude, and creative ability that may be totally lacking in them at other times.

The emotion of sex cannot be entirely submerged, but it can be sublimated and diverted in such a way that it becomes an irresistible power for action behind one's major purpose.

The third motive: *the desire for material gain*. This desire is fundamental in human nature. If you can combine these first three—the emotion of love, the emotion of sex, and the desire for material wealth—you will have named the three emotions that make the world go round. You may be sure that if you are motivated by this combination, you will not be watching the clock. You will be much more anxious to get to the job than you are to get through with it and away from it, and you will not feel that work is a burden.

At this point I want to say something about money and other forms of material wealth. Many people let a fear of poverty ruin their chances to enjoy the other riches of life. The real good in money consists of the use to which it is put, not the mere possession of it. I have learned that true happiness is not found in the possession of things but in the privilege of self-expression through the use of material things. I have found out in life that you must have money, and have an abundance of it, in order to enjoy freedom of body and mind—a choice blessing. A person cannot be really free if he must be chained to a routine job most of his waking hours and receive in return for that a mere subsistence. If a person has to pay that much for existence, he is paying too high a price.

I am in the business of getting people to break with their past habits of accepting the crumbs from life's table and teaching them a proven way of ridding themselves of self-imposed limitations and enjoying their fill of life's riches.

The fourth motive: *the desire for self-preservation.* Everyone, of course, is motivated in this direction.

The fifth motive: *the desire for freedom of body and mind.* Basic within everyone's heart is the desire to be free and unfettered. Ask the average man you meet, and he will tell you that someday he's going to be his own boss, and nobody is going to tell him what to do.

The sixth motive: *the desire for self-expression and recognition.* There is a rather peculiar principle connected with this desire: the things you give to others through expression are the only things you are able to retain, remember, or keep for yourself. Any gems of thought or wisdom that you are anxious to remember you must repeatedly give to others, or they will elude your grasp at a crucial moment.

I am suggesting the sharing of the principles of this philosophy with others (although not the details of your purpose or plans, which you are cautioned to keep strictly to yourself). Giving is a form of expression, and giving is living. No one ever achieved outstanding success without the cooperation of others, and of course you must give something in return for this cooperation. Therein lies the strategic importance of the desire for self-expression and recognition.

The seventh motive: *life after death*. This is a very strong motive. A desire for perpetual life is closely allied with the desire for self-preservation and is instinctive in the nature of humanity.

The eighth motive: *the desire for revenge*. Although the feeling of getting even with someone is basic to humans, it is the primitive law of the jungle, and it is utterly wasteful. If you must get even, get even with the ones who have helped you.

The ninth motive: the emotion of *fear*. There are seven basic fears, some combination of which every human suffers at one time or another. Fear can rob you of your personal initiative and help keep you in poverty all through life. All of the basic fears must be conquered if you are going to eliminate their negative influence.

Now let me introduce you to your other self, that power within you that is yours and for which you need no person other than yourself, the power you have as an individual to contact Infinite Intelligence for the solution to your problems. It is a power so great that you can get anything you want in life by using it. Nor will I qualify that: I used to say, "within reason," but now I say that whatever you want in life you are capable of obtaining.

I'm very happy now to come to the how-to division of this chapter, wherein I shall give you detailed step-by-step instruction in applying these principles in the attainment of your own plans and purposes.

1. Write out a definite, clear, concise plan by which you intend to achieve your definite major purpose. State the maximum amount of time you are allowing for the fulfillment of your desire. Break the achievement down into units of effort that are in the realm of possibility and probability.

2. Describe exactly what you intend to give in return for the realization of your purpose.

3. There is no such reality as something for nothing. Everything has a price tag on it, and you must be willing to read the price tag and to pay it in full before you get the object of your desire. This price must usu-

ally be paid in advance. It is possible to pay it on the installment plan and in easy steps, but the total price must be paid before the object of your desire becomes your own.

4. Make your plan flexible so as to permit change. Your definite major purpose, if it is really that, will not change until it is fulfilled, but the plan for achieving that purpose may change many times. Infinite Intelligence may reveal to you a plan that is far superior for your purpose to the one you dreamed up. Stand ready at all times to receive, accept gladly and gratefully, and willingly adopt any better plans which occur to your mind out of the blue.

5. Remember to call your major purpose and your plans into your conscious mind as often as may be practical. Eat with them, sleep with them, take them with you wherever you go. Bear in mind the fact that your subconscious mind can thus be influenced to work for the attainment of your major purpose while you are asleep. Keep your mind on the things that you want and off the things that you don't want until your major purpose becomes a burning desire.

Remember: whatever the mind can conceive and believe, it can achieve. Vividly visualize in your mind your definite major purpose and your other real desires or goals. Each time you imagine a goal, repeat these words ten times:

→ *I vividly visualize myself as the person I want to be, and I am enthusiastically achieving my goals.*

→ *I vividly visualize myself as the person I want to be, and I am enthusiastically achieving my goals.*

→ *I vividly visualize myself as the person I want to be, and I am enthusiastically achieving my goals.*

→ *I vividly visualize myself as the person I want to be, and I am enthusiastically achieving my goals.*

→ *I vividly visualize myself as the person I want to be, and I am enthusiastically achieving my goals.*

→ *I vividly visualize myself as the person I want to be, and I am enthusiastically achieving my goals.*

→ *I vividly visualize myself as the person I want to be, and I am enthusiastically achieving my goals.*

→ *I vividly visualize myself as the person I want to be, and I am enthusiastically achieving my goals.*

→ *I vividly visualize myself as the person I want to be, and I am enthusiastically achieving my goals.*

→ *I vividly visualize myself as the person I want to be, and I am enthusiastically achieving my goals.*

2

The Master Mind Alliance

The Master Mind principle makes it possible for an individual, through association with others, to acquire and utilize all of the knowledge needed for attaining any desired goal.

To begin with, the Master Mind principle consists of an alliance of two or more minds working in perfect harmony for the attainment of a definite objective. No one has ever attained outstanding success in the upper bracket of any calling without applying the Master Mind Principle. This is because no one mind is complete by itself. All truly great minds have been reinforced through contacts with other minds. Every mind needs association and contact with other minds in order to grow and expand.

Sometimes this reinforcement or amplification takes place accidentally, without the individual's awareness of what is happening or how it is happening. The very greatest minds, however, are the result of deliberate understanding and use of this Master Mind Principle, which may be one reason why there are few truly great Master Minds.

Several fundamental principles are connected with the subject. The first one is that the Master Mind principle is a practical medium through which you may appropriate and use the full benefits of the experience, training, education, specialized knowledge, and native intelligence of other people as completely as if they were your own. Now isn't this a wonderful privilege? You can use the expert knowledge of such allies as geologists, chemists, other scientists, the accumulated knowledge of mankind, and of course the entire philosophy of the science of personal achievement.

The second principle is harmony. An active alliance of two or more minds in a spirit of perfect harmony for the attainment of a common objective stimulates each mind to a higher degree of courage than ordinarily experienced and paves the way for that state of mind known as *faith*. There must be a complete meeting of the minds, without reservation on the part of any member. There must be accord in the facts, agreement in the opinions, and an absolute community of interest in the definite objective. Each member of the alliance must subordinate his own personal ambitions to the fulfillment and successful achievement of the definite purpose of the alliance.

Now this kind of harmony is not achieved immediately. It is cultivated and grows based upon these four elements: (1) confidence, (2) understanding, (3) fairness, and (4) justice.

Confidence is reliance or assurance based on fidelity. The purpose of the alliance should never be discussed outside the ranks of the members, unless this purpose happens to be the performance of some public service.

Understanding means the complete knowledge of the nature, significance, and implications of a situation or proposition and to have a tolerant or sympathetic attitude toward it. Each member of the alliance must be in sympathy with the definite purpose that is undertaken. Each one agrees that it is a good idea and one to which he will give wholehearted support.

Fairness indicates the absence of any partiality, favor, or prejudice. It also shows freedom from bias and selfishness.

Justice implies that no one member of the alliance is seeking unfair advantage or selfish purpose at the expense of the other members.

Every mind is equipped to both send and receive thought vibrations. This process of communication between the minds of individuals is going around all the time, although they are rarely conscious of the fact. This truth has great significance in connection with the Master Mind principles. It has been proved conclusively that a mind whose alertness has been increased through Master Mind stimulation, becomes much more receptive to thoughts released by other minds than it would be under normal circumstances. Likewise, the mind of the individual thus stimulated has greater power to project the thought vibrations of his own mind to the minds of others.

Nature's building blocks are available to man in the form of thought energy. When two or more minds coordinate their thinking in a spirit of harmony and work toward a definite objective, they place themselves in a position to absorb power directly from the great universal storehouse of Infinite Intelligence. This is the greatest of all sources of power.

Now here is an important consideration: one man with a negative attitude can influence a thousand others in an organization without ever saying a word. The medium of contact is telepathy. Your mind is constantly in tune with every other mind within its range, whatever that range happens to be. Some minds have a much longer range than others. You are constantly picking up the thoughts of other people and often mistaking them for your own thoughts. This is why you cannot afford to remain in a negative atmosphere unless you have a technique for protecting your mind from these negative broadcasts.

Whatever you are going to ask the members of your Master Mind alliance to do for you, you must condition your own mind to do first. Never, under any circumstances, try to operate a Master Mind while you are negative. Get out of the presence of your Master Mind allies, and stay out until you make yourself positive. You see, states of mind are contagious. Be sure the things you are passing on to other people are positive and not negative, because they will reflect back to you and react according to the state of mind that you send out to them.

It is highly important to condition your mind so that when you speak to others, not only will your words be heard, but the feeling behind them will go along too. Sometimes your mental attitudes will put over your message better than your words. There is really no way to express some of the subtleties of mental intercourse other than by means of the spirit behind your words.

Remember: success and failure are in your own mind. Once you are awakened by this stupendous realization, you will have at your disposal the twelve great riches of life:

1. A positive mental attitude
2. Sound physical health
3. Harmony in human relationships
4. Freedom from fear

5. The hope of achievement

6. The capacity for faith

7. The willingness to share one's blessings

8. A labor of love

9. A mind that is open to all subjects

10. Self-discipline

11. The capacity to understand people

12. Financial security

Man's greatest Master Mind alliance is that with the woman he loves. Thus it is essential to nourish that love by keeping the spark of romance alive. The thrill of romance takes the drudgery from toil. It raises the thoughts of the humblest worker to the status of genius. It drives away discouragement and replaces it with definiteness of purpose. It transforms poverty into a mighty stimulus and an irresistible power for achievement. It is the very essence of enthusiasm and fires the imagination, forcing it to creative action.

The emotion of sex is nature's own source of inspiration, through which she gives both men and women the impelling desire to create, build, lead, and direct. Men of vision, initiative, and enthusiasm who lead and excel in art, music, drama, industry, and business express the emotion of sex transmuted into human behavior, and they owe their superiority to this fact. The spirit of romance, as well as devotion to the object of a man's affection, is a great driving force which may be used in the pursuit of a his calling. The force that is born of a combination of love and sex is the very elixir of life, through which nature expresses all creative effort. The married man who is on the right terms with his wife—terms of complete harmony, understanding, sympathy, and singleness of purpose—has a priceless asset in this relationship, which may lift him to great heights of personal achievement.

As we have seen, love heads the list of the nine basic motives of life that inspire all voluntary actions of people. When love abounds as the basis of the family Master Mind relationship, the family finances will not be likely to give cause for disturbance, for love has a way of surmounting all obstacles, meeting all problems, and overcoming all difficulties.

Other types of alliances are educational, religious, political, social, and economic. A mind that remains brilliant, alert, receptive, and flexible must constantly have the companionship of other minds. No man can achieve greatness alone. Every outstanding success is based on cooperative effort.

The first step in forming and maintaining a Master Mind alliance is to adopt a definite purpose to be attained by the alliance, choosing individual members whose education, experience, and influence are such as to make them of the greatest value in achieving that purpose. Do not choose people simply because you know them and like them; each member of the alliance should make some definite, distinctive, and unique contribution to the overall picture. You should be guided in your choice by the things you need that you do not already have. The number of individuals in an alliance should be governed entirely by the nature and magnitude of the purpose to be obtained. Determine what appropriate benefit each member may receive in return for his cooperation in the alliance. If you make a profit, be willing to divide it with those who help you. Be not only fair but generous with them. Remember the principle of going the extra mile.

Establish a definite place where the members of the alliance will meet. Have a definite plan and arrange a definite time for the mutual discussion of the plan. It is important that frequent and regular contacts be made between the members. It is the burden of the leader of the alliance to see that harmony among all the members is maintained and that action is continuous in the pursuance of the definite major objective.

Action or work is a connecting link between desire, plan, and fulfillment. The watchword of the alliance should be *definiteness*: definiteness of purpose and positiveness of plans, backed by continuous perfect harmony.

Definiteness of purpose is the first element that interlocks with the Master Mind principle. Then you must have personal initiative. You must take the lead. You can't wait for somebody else to come along and help you out. You also need applied faith and the practice of going the extra mile. Self-discipline is indispensable. Don't try to discipline others, but discipline yourself. You cannot succeed in life by scattering your forces and trying to do a dozen things at the same time. You have to concentrate on one thing.

An all-wise Providence has so arranged the mechanism of the mind that no single mind is complete. Richness of mind in its fullest sense comes from the harmonious alliance of two or more minds working together towards the achievement of some definite purpose. Among the factors that enable an individual to rise above mediocrity is an understanding of the power that is available to the person who blends his mind power with that of other people, thereby giving himself the full benefit of an intangible force which no single mind can ever experience. No two minds ever come into contact without bringing into existence a third and intangible mind—a greater power than either of the two minds.

The Master Mind principle is not a man-made principle. It is part of the great system of natural law. It is as immutable as the law of gravitation, which holds the stars and the planets in their places, and as definite in every phase of its operation. We may not be able to influence this law, but we can understand it and adapt

ourselves to it in ways that will bring us great benefits no matter who we are or what our calling may be.
Success is the power to get whatever one desires in life
without violating the rights of others. Knowledge alone
is not power; power is the appropriation and use of
other men's knowledge and experience for the attainment of some definite purpose. Moreover, it is power of
the most beneficial order.

Think of the positive-minded people that you would
like to have as your consultants and associates. Imagine
being with this capable, positive-minded group in perfect harmony, helping to map and plan the achieving of
your goals and now say:

→ *I like to meet in harmony with my positive-minded
   friends to Master Mind my goals.*

→ *I like to meet in harmony with my positive-minded
   friends to Master Mind my goals.*

→ *I like to meet in harmony with my positive-minded
   friends to Master Mind my goals.*

→ *I like to meet in harmony with my positive-minded
   friends to Master Mind my goals.*

→ *I like to meet in harmony with my positive-minded
   friends to Master Mind my goals.*

→ *I like to meet in harmony with my positive-minded
   friends to Master Mind my goals.*

→ *I like to meet in harmony with my positive-minded
   friends to Master Mind my goals.*

→ *I like to meet in harmony with my positive-minded friends to Master Mind my goals.*

→ *I like to meet in harmony with my positive-minded friends to Master Mind my goals.*

→ *I like to meet in harmony with my positive-minded friends to Master Mind my goals.*

3

The Meaning of Faith

The purpose of this chapter is to describe the exact meaning of faith, with suggestions for applying it to solve your daily problems. I am talking about the active motivating faith that you can put into daily practice without regard to any form of theology or religion. The only religion I intend to deal with is the broad general religion of right thinking and right living as you meet important human relationships in the real situations of life.

The real difficulty in defining faith is that it is a state of mind. Furthermore, it is not a passive state of mind, where the mind is merely giving assent, but an active state. The mind is in the state of relating itself to the great external élan vital or vital force of the universe.

The word *faith* is an abstract idea, a purely mental conception. That's why it is not better understood. The only way it can be understood is to see someone or something real, tangible, or concrete doing something or expressing something.

In the case of faith, the real, tangible thing is man using his mind to sense the powers that surround him in this wonderful world and trying to harmonize his life with those thrilling powers as he feels them. This, the relationship between the mind of man and the unseen powers of the universe, is infinite in its possibilities; therein lies the difficulty of saying exactly what faith is.

In the final analysis, faith is the activity of individual minds facing themselves and establishing a working association with a power variously referred to as the universal mind, the great unseen, the divine mind, or, by the more orthodox religionists, as God, and by the students of this philosophy as Infinite Intelligence.

At this point I wish to explain just what I mean by Infinite Intelligence, because it is my opinion that no one may ever reach the state of mind called faith without a positive, definite belief in a Supreme Being. In arriving at this conviction, you may employ every faculty you possess: observation, experimentation, feeling, prayer, meditation, and thought are all legitimate approaches.

To thinking man, the external universe has always been evidence of the existence of a supreme, creative, directing power. The advance of science reveals many secrets of the workings of this power, which we call *nature*. Every process of nature is orderly. No chance, no disorder or chaos has been seen in the physical universe. The sun does not rise in the east today, the west tomorrow. All of the phenomena of nature are products of law. Not a single exception has thus far been found. The universe exists under a reign of perfect order and law. Such prevalent order, such obedience to law, clearly implies intelligent planning and definiteness of purpose.

Order is the product of intelligent direction. Sober men of science today declare that the universe appears as a product of thought. The conclusion is inescapable. There can be no planning or purpose without a mind. There can be no thought without a thinker. The universe declares that there is intelligent purpose in nature; therefore there must be a supreme Infinite Intelligence directing it.

Take a look at the wristwatch on your arm. You know who made it, you can learn how it operates, you can analyze the metal of its parts. You know also that your watch did not come into existence without the aid of organized intelligence, and you know that the particular intelligence in this case is the mind of man. Equally well you know that the intelligence the man used did not originate in his mind; he was merely an instrument expressing the creative force of a greater intelligence. If you take the watch apart, separating the parts from their correct working relationships to each other, put them in a hat and shake them, never in a million years would they—nor could they—reassemble themselves into the same functioning machine called a watch. Your watch operates accurately only because there is organized intelligence and a definite plan behind it. Therefore it is reasonable to have faith in an organized Infinite Intelligence behind the operations of the universe, which our senses describe to us.

You may develop faith by conditioning your mind to receive Infinite Intelligence. Applied faith is adapting the power received from Infinite Intelligence to a definite major purpose. Applied faith has been called the dynamo of this entire philosophy because applied faith will give you the power to put the philosophy into action. The word *dynamo*, as you know, is just another name for a generator of electrical power. Faith is the state of mind wherein you temporarily relax your reason and willpower and open your mind completely to the guidance of Infinite Intelligence for the attainment of some definite purpose. The guidance comes in the form of an idea or a plan that comes to you while you are in this receptive attitude.

The mind has been cleverly provided with a gateway of approach to Infinite Intelligence through what is known as the *subconscious*. The subconscious mind, according to the best evidence available, is the gateway between the conscious mind of man and the vast reservoir of Infinite Intelligence. It might be likened to a spigot or a valve through which flows the stream of intelligence upon which we depend for our growth and development and the unfolding of our innate powers. It is in this inflowing stream of intelligence that we live and move and have our being. We must therefore keep this gateway open. We must keep it free from self-imposed limitations and restrictions. We must do nothing that might dam up this inflowing energy.

Infinite Intelligence recognizes no limitations except those we impose upon ourselves. The idea of man's mind being an instrument for the reception and distribution of the power of Infinite Intelligence is basic to an understanding of applied faith. Whatsoever the mind of man can conceive and believe it can achieve, so long as it does not run counter to any natural laws and is in harmony with the morals of the orderly universe.

At least one of the purposes of man's existence here on earth seems to be to act as the receiver and distributor of the power of Infinite Intelligence. To the extent that man cooperates in this purpose, he allies himself with the forces behind all nature; conversely, to the extent that he looks out only for his own selfish ends, he is opposing this power or retarding its flow. The power of Infinite Intelligence pours life into us as the flowing stream, maintaining all of the functions of our bodies and minds. We can use this energy to guide and govern circumstances and conditions of our lives if we will act as its conductors and shape it according to our constructive purposes. This inflowing power has no limitations or defects, but it is forced to manifest itself in this world in a way we as individuals can understand and express.

If you would have faith, keep your mind on what you want and off what you do not want. What do you want? Make up your mind precisely what you want through definiteness of purpose; then apply the power of your faith to it. Like the perfect flower, which lies latent in the unopened bud, the seed of your burning desire needs only the sunshine of your faith to start germinating. You acquire this power of faith by utilizing the instrument of contact with Infinite Intelligence, which is your subconscious mind. You activate your subconscious mind and focus this power upon the accomplishment of your purposes by continually bombarding it with a clear-cut statement of those purposes while you are in a state of high emotion.

Here is a tremendous idea for you to think over: the creative force of the entire universe functions through your mind when you establish a definite purpose and apply your faith to its fulfillment. The one sure, infallible way to separate yourself from the mass of humanity and climb out of the level of the average and mediocre is not to journey to some desert or forgotten island or lock yourself in solitary confinement, but to hitch your wagon to the star of some very strong purpose. In this way you pull yourself out of the mass of self-centered, self-seeking, negative humanity and ally yourself with the great life-giving force of Infinite Intelligence.

I cannot overemphasize the importance of silent meditation. This form of concentrated thinking activates your subconscious mind and accelerates its vibratory rate so as to more efficiently establish contact between your conscious mind and Infinite Intelligence. This is the way to take possession of your own mind and tap this inexhaustible source of power.

You should set a definite period of not less than one hour out of the twenty-four for engaging in deep serious thought about your relationship with Infinite Intelligence. This investment of time will pay you dividends that will enrich your life beyond your present dreams. If you happen to be a religious person, you can make this a period of prayer. I think, though, as you read on, you will get a slightly different idea of prayer than is held by the average individual.

From what I have said, it must be obvious that faith is a state of mind that you can attain only by properly clearing your mind of all negative thoughts of want, poverty, fear, ill-health, and disharmony. When you have cleared your mind of these negative thoughts, there are three easy steps you can take to create the state of mind known as faith. They are:

1. Express a definite desire for the achievement of the purpose. Relate it to one or more of the basic motives.
2. Create a definite and specific plan for the attainment of that desire.
3. Start acting on that plan, putting every conscious effort behind it.

Since Infinite Intelligence is available to the subconscious, if there are better and more perfect plans, you will be inspired by a hunch or intuition to change the plans you have made. This procedure places your spiritual strength squarely back of your desire and hands the problem over to your Creator. When the solution of your problem comes, as it surely will if you rely upon your faith in the infinite, it will come as an idea or a plan transmitted to your conscious mind by the subconscious, which is the doorway to infinite power.

Never mind what your reason tells you about this mode of procedure. In conditioning your mind to receive Infinite Intelligence so that it can guide you, you have temporarily subdued your faculty of reason. This part of the instructions is very important. Unless you can willingly follow it, your reason will challenge you at every step, and you will not be able to relax your will and submit yourself entirely to the higher powers that you are seeking. You will need some practice to acquire this art of conditioning your mind to be receptive.

You may wonder how you will know when you have an answer. You will come to recognize the soundness of this plan and the authenticity of its power by the feeling of intense enthusiasm that accompanies this inspiration. When the plan comes through to your conscious mind, accept it with appreciation and gratitude, and act on it at once. Do not hesitate; do not argue, challenge, worry, or fret about it or wonder if it's right. Act on it.

Here is a further word about prayer: if you will make your prayers an expression of gratitude and thanksgiving for the blessings you have already received instead of importuning for what you do not have, you will find that you obtain results a great deal faster. Do not expect Infinite Intelligence to bring you the physical equivalent of your desire. Accept with gratitude a plan for fulfilling your desires according to the usual rules of human conduct. Do not look for miracles. Infinite Intelligence prefers to work through natural laws, employing whatever physical means are available.

The worst enemy of mankind is fear. You cannot exercise the pure clean power of faith, which is Infinite Intelligence expressing itself in your life, as long as there is one iota of fear or worry in your mind about anything. You have to learn to give your mind a mental bath, and no matter what the price is, go through with it. That is the first step in conditioning your mind for faith. Get rid of the things that are causing you to be afraid. Faith and fear cannot exist in the heart at the same time.

A one-sentence definition of faith is: it is the art of believing by doing. The doing, of course, is the big secret. Faith can exist only so long as it is being used. Just as you cannot develop a muscular arm by disuse, you cannot develop faith by merely talking and thinking about it.

Two words are inseparably associated with faith: *persistence* and *action*. Faith comes as a result of putting persistent action behind definiteness of purpose. Strong purpose and a sound motive clear the mind of many doubts and fears and other negatives, which must be removed in order to permit faith to operate. When you desire anything and pursue that desire actively, you will soon find your mind opening automatically for the guidance of faith. Faith without works is dead.

The emergencies of life often bring individuals to the crossroads where they are forced to choose their direction, one road being marked "faith" and the other "fear." What causes the vast majority to take the fear road? The choice hinges upon one's mental attitude. The man who takes the fear road does so because he has neglected to condition his mind to be positive. What if you have failed in the past? So what? So did Edison. So did Henry Ford, the Wright brothers, Andrew Carnegie, and all other great leaders who have helped to establish the American way of life. With the aid of the light that shines from within, these and all truly great men have recognized temporary defeat for exactly what it is: a challenge to great effort backed by greater faith. Just as a single drop of water out of the ocean is an integral part of the ocean, know that you too are a part of the universal purpose of Infinite Intelligence.

So repeat these words:

→ *I have complete faith and trust in Infinite Intelligence, and I know that I am achieving my goals.*

→ *I have complete faith and trust in Infinite Intelligence, and I know that I am achieving my goals.*

→ *I have complete faith and trust in Infinite Intelligence, and I know that I am achieving my goals.*

→ *I have complete faith and trust in Infinite Intelligence, and I know that I am achieving my goals.*

→ *I have complete faith and trust in Infinite Intelligence, and I know that I am achieving my goals.*

→ *I have complete faith and trust in Infinite Intelligence, and I know that I am achieving my goals.*

→ *I have complete faith and trust in Infinite Intelligence, and I know that I am achieving my goals.*

→ *I have complete faith and trust in Infinite Intelligence, and I know that I am achieving my goals.*

→ *I have complete faith and trust in Infinite Intelligence, and I know that I am achieving my goals.*

→ *I have complete faith and trust in Infinite Intelligence, and I know that I am achieving my goals.*

4

The Thirty Traits of a Pleasing Personality

Personality is the sum total of the mental, spiritual, and physical traits and habits that distinguish an individual from all others. It is the factor which, more than anything else, determines whether one is liked or disliked by others.

It's very encouraging for one to know that the thirty traits of a pleasing personality are within the reach of the humblest person and that they may be had for a reasonable price, which works no hardship on anyone. Here they are:

1. **A positive mental attitude.** Inasmuch as a positive mental attitude heads the list of traits of a pleasing personality and also heads the list of the twelve

riches, let us examine the qualities which lead to the development of this very desirable quality.

What one looks for in others one finds eventually mirrored in his own character; therefore the habit of looking for the good in others leads to the development of good in oneself. One must recognize that nothing is worth the cost of worry and that there are two types of worries: (1) those one may correct, and (2) those over which one has no control and about which one can do nothing. Deliberately filling the mind with positive thoughts and refusing space to negative thoughts provides the mind with a positive consciousness that inspires the individual to think in positive terms on all subjects. Self-analysis must begin with strict self-discipline based upon the courage to recognize one's faults and a sincere desire to eliminate them.

2. **Flexibility of mind**. Flexibility consists of the habit of adapting oneself to quickly changing circumstances without losing composure. The person who maintains a positive mental attitude will have no difficulty in maintaining flexibility of personality, because a positive mind is always under control and may be directed at will to any desired purpose.

3. **Sincerity of purpose**. This is one trait for which a satisfactory substitute never has been found, because it reaches deeper into a human being than most of the

other personal qualities. Sincerity begins with one-self, and it is a trait of sound character that reflects itself so visibly that none can fail to observe it.

Be sincere first of all with yourself. Be sincere with those to whom you are related by family ties. Be sincere with your daily associates in connection with your occupation. Be sincere with your friends and acquaintances and, of course, with your country. Above all, be sincere with the giver of all gifts to mankind.

4. **Promptness of decision**. All successful men reach decisions quickly. Many of them become annoyed by those who do not act promptly. Promptness of decisions is a habit one must form through self-discipline. Those who have the vision to recognize opportunity and the promptness of decision necessary to embrace it will get ahead, but no others will.

5. **Common courtesy**. Courtesy is the habit of rendering useful service without the expectation of direct reward; respecting other people's feelings under all circumstances; going out of one's way, if need be, to help any less fortunate person when and wherever possible; and last but not least, controlling selfishness, greed, envy, and hatred.

6. **A pleasing tone of voice**. The spoken word is the medium by which one most often expresses one's personality. The tone of voice, therefore, should be

so definitely under control that it can be colored and modified so as to make it convey any desired meaning quite in addition to the words used. As your voice is the most direct expression of your innermost self, you should be very careful to do yourself full justice with it.

7. **The habit of smiling**. This habit, like many others, is directly related to the individual's mental attitude, and it discloses the nature of his mental attitude almost perfectly. The man who desires to improve his personality should devote a definite amount of time each day to practicing before a mirror until he is able to harmonize the tone of his voice with his smile. The habit will pay big dividends on the time devoted to it.

8. **Facial expression**. Men have no tails for wagging, but they do have muscles that control the lines of their faces, and these muscles serve the same purpose. A smile produces one arrangement of these lines, while a frown produces an entirely different arrangement, but each conveys with unerring accuracy the feeling that is taking place within the mind. Thus the smile, the tone of voice, and the expression on the face constitute open windows through which all who will may see and feel what takes place in the minds of people.

9. **Tactfulness**. Tactfulness consists of doing and saying the right thing at the right time. There are many

ways in which people show their lack of tact, but the following are among the more common: (a) carelessness in the tone of voice, often resulting in gruff and irritable tones, indicating that the speaker is displeased or in a negative mental attitude; (b) the habit of speaking out of turn when silence would be more appropriate; (c) interrupting the speech of others, one of the most frequent expressions of discourtesy, and also indicating a lack of culture; (d) overworking the personal pronoun *I*; (e) volunteering opinions that have not been requested and for which no reason exists, especially on subjects with which one is not familiar; (f) presuming upon friendship or acquaintanceship in asking favors one has not earned the right to request; (g) expressing one's dislike too freely.

10. **Tolerance**. Tolerance consists of an open mind on all subjects toward all people at all times. In addition to being one of the more important of the traits of a pleasing personality, an open mind on all subjects is one of the twelve great riches of life.

11. **Frankness in manner and speech**. Individuals of sound character always have the courage to deal directly and openly with others, and they follow this habit even though it may at times be to their disadvantage. Perhaps their greatest compensation consists in being able to maintain a clear conscience.

12. **A keen sense of humor**. A well-developed sense of humor aids an individual in becoming flexible and adjustable to the varying circumstances of life. It also enables him to relax and, of course, to become more human. Moreover, a keen sense of humor keeps one from taking oneself and life too seriously, a tendency toward which many people are inclined.

13. **Faith in Infinite Intelligence**. Faith in Infinite Intelligence inspires faith in other things as well, while doubt begets doubt. Faith is the master gate through which one may give one's brain free access to the great universal power of thought. Faith must inevitably be woven into every principle of the philosophy of individual achievement, because the intangible power of faith is the essence of every great achievement, no matter what may be its nature or source.

14. **A keen sense of justice**. Justice, as the term is used here, refers to intentional honesty. The individual so rigidly adheres to this deliberate honesty that he is motivated by it under all circumstances.

15. **Appropriateness of words**. The English language is replete with words that carry every conceivable shade of meaning; hence there can be no valid excuse for the common habit of using words that offend the sensibilities of others. And of course the use of profanity at any time or under any circumstances is wholly inexcusable.

16. **Control of the emotions**. Control of the emotions can be attained through one of the twelve riches, self-discipline, and it is necessary for enjoying the benefits of a pleasing personality. Some of the feelings that must be brought under control are, on the negative side, fear, hatred, anger, envy, greed, jealousy, revenge, irritability, and superstition. On the positive side, they are love, sex, faith, hope, desire, loyalty, sympathy, and optimism.

17. **Alertness of interest**. One can pay another no greater compliment than concentrating one's attention upon that person's personal interest. It is a greater accomplishment to be an attentive listener when another is speaking than to be an able speaker.

18. **Effective speech**. We have only to observe carefully to find men who have risen to great heights of personal achievement because of their ability to sell themselves and their ideas through dramatic speech. The most important factor in effective speech is a thorough knowledge of the subject about which one speaks. The greatest of all rules of effective speaking can be stated in one sentence: know what you wish to say, say it with all the emotional feeling at your command, and then sit down.

19. **Versatility**. The more popular types of people are very versatile. They have at least a surface knowledge of many subjects. They are interested in other peo-

ple and their ideas, and they go out of their way to express that interest when it will inspire appropriate reaction.

20. **A fondness for people**. People who dislike others will inevitably be disliked. Through the principle of telepathy, every mind communicates with all other minds within its range. The person who wishes to develop an attractive personality is under the constant necessity of controlling not only his words and deeds but his thoughts as well.

21. **Control of temper**. The man who lets his temper fly in all directions is sure to find it alighting where it will do him great injury on the rebound. Perhaps the greatest injury an uncontrolled temper may do is from an uncontrolled tongue. Emotion under control, however, is one of the greatest of all powers available to humanity.

22. **Hope and ambition**. A man without an ambition or the hope of achieving it may be harmless to others, but he will never be popular. No one cares very much about a person who shows clearly by his deeds, or lack of deeds, that he has abandoned hope of getting ahead in this world.

23. **Temperance**. The man who lacks the necessary self-discipline to manage his personal habits instead of being controlled by them is never attractive to others. This is especially true of the habits of eating, drink-

ing, and sexual relationships. Excesses in relation to any of these destroy personal magnetism.

24. **Patience**. This is a fast-moving, high-speed world, and the tempo of human thoughts and deeds is so rapid that people often get into one another's way; therefore patience is required to avoid the destructive effects of friction in human relationships.

25. **Humility of the heart**. This is the outgrowth of understanding of man's relationship to his Creator, plus the recognition that the material blessings of life are gifts from the Creator for the common good of all mankind. The man who is on good terms with his own conscience and his Creator always is humble at heart, no matter how many of the material riches of life he may have accumulated or what his personal achievements may be.

26. **Appropriateness of personal adornment**. The best-dressed person is usually the one whose clothes and accessories are so well chosen and whose entire ensemble so well harmonized that the individual does not attract undue attention because of his or her personal adornment.

27. **Effective showmanship**. Effective showmanship combines many of the other traits of a pleasing personality, such as facial expression, control of the tone of voice, appropriate personal adornment, proper choice of words, mastery of the emotions, courtesy,

effective speech, versatility, a positive mental attitude, a keen sense of humor, alertness of interest in other people, and tactfulness.

28. **Clean sportsmanship**. Clean sportsmanship is an important trait of an attractive personality because it inspires people to cooperate in a friendly manner. Indicative of sound character, it hardly needs further endorsement.

29. **The ability to shake hands properly**. Many people might never think of handshaking as having anything to do with a pleasing personality, but in fact it has a great deal to do with the subject. The person who shakes hands properly coordinates his handshake with his words of greeting, generally emphasizing each word with a firm grip of the hand—not a viselike squeeze—and does not release the other person's hand until he finishes the spoken greeting.

30. **Personal magnetism**. Let's frankly admit at the outset that *personal magnetism* is a very polite way of describing sex emotion, for that is precisely what it means. Sex emotion is the power behind all creative vision. It is the means by which all living species are perpetuated. It inspires the use of the imagination, enthusiasm, and personal initiative. There has never been born a great leader in any calling who was not motivated in part by the creative powers of sex emotion.

* * *

A man's personality is his greatest asset or his greatest liability, for it embraces everything that he controls: his mind, body, and soul. A man's personality is the man himself. It shapes the nature of his thoughts, his deeds, and his relationships with others, and establishes the boundaries of the space that he occupies in the world.

Visualize yourself as a loving friend to everyone, radiating warmth, affection, and friendship. You are genuinely interested in them and their welfare. Now repeat these words:

→ *I like people, and I radiate warmth and friendship to all.*
→ *I like people, and I radiate warmth and friendship to all.*
→ *I like people, and I radiate warmth and friendship to all.*
→ *I like people, and I radiate warmth and friendship to all.*
→ *I like people, and I radiate warmth and friendship to all.*
→ *I like people, and I radiate warmth and friendship to all.*
→ *I like people, and I radiate warmth and friendship to all.*
→ *I like people, and I radiate warmth and friendship to all.*
→ *I like people, and I radiate warmth and friendship to all.*
→ *I like people, and I radiate warmth and friendship to all.*

5

Going the Extra Mile

I'm going to make a promise to you who study this chapter and put its principles into practice as a matter of habit: if you will immediately start rendering more and better service than that for which you are presently paid, you will be rewarded in several definite ways:

1. You will sooner or later receive compensation far exceeding the actual value of the service you render.

2. In addition to this material gain, you will exhibit greater strength of character in other ways.

3. You will find that it is easier for you to maintain a positive mental attitude at all times.

4. You will experience the thrill of new and stronger convictions of courage and self-reliance, new surges

of the self-starting power of personal initiative, and an energizing influx of vital enthusiasm.

5. Finally, you will find that there is a permanent market for your services, and because of your reputation you will not be out of a job.

Does this sound to you like a big order for one chapter to deliver? True enough, it is a big order, but the power behind this strategic principle can fill the order and give you extra measure as well. This principle was observed and commented upon hundreds of years before the dawn of the Christian era, but one of the most classic expressions of it appears in the essay entitled "Compensation" by Ralph Waldo Emerson.

There is a rather subtle but powerful *something* connected with the observance of this principle which must be sensed or felt or discerned intuitively. The degree to which you are able to capture this attitude will determine your success in achieving the promises made above.

One thing I mean by going the extra mile is, don't wait for people to tell you to do something, because that takes a lot of the kick out of doing it. Tell yourself to jump in and do it.

If you have the right attitude in the things you do for people, you will be successful in putting them under obligation. If you don't have the right attitude, they will suspect you of something, dislike you, and find an excuse for not reciprocating.

There is no better place to start this discussion than by showing how nature herself forces every living creature to observe this principle or perish—except humans. Humans, of all creatures, have the right of choice either to disobey the law and suffer the consequences or obey the law and reap the rewards.

You will find that Mother Nature goes the extra mile in everything she does. She doesn't create just barely enough of each genus or species to get by; she produces an overabundance to take care of all emergencies that arise and still have enough left to guarantee the perpetuation of each form of life.

Each spring, look at the blooms on the fruit trees. Here nature makes allowances for the winds and storms and unusual frosts that may destroy many of the blooms by having enough blooms left to produce a crop of fruit. There, you see, nature does go the extra mile, simply by producing an abundance of blooms, which attract the bees. The bees go the extra mile by rendering their services before they are compensated. The result is the production of fruit and the perpetuation of the bees.

Here are two very important laws. They are important because they deal with your life and the things with which you would become familiar. One is *the law of compensation*, the other *the law of increasing returns*. Mankind depends for its very life upon the operation of these two laws, for if the farmer did not comply with them, he could produce no food.

Let's take a look at the farmer. See how he must necessarily observe these laws of life, plus the principle of going the extra mile, whether he consciously recognizes it or not. First, the farmer must clear the soil of trees and shrubs, then he must plow, harrow, and fertilize where necessary. After this, he must sow the soil with seed. He must mix intelligence with his labor, observing the proper season of the year for planting, the correct method of crop culture, and the right irrigation and cultivation techniques. If the farmer has performed his labor intelligently, nature will reward him through the law of compensation, by which she neither permits any living thing to get something for nothing nor allows any form of labor to go unrewarded. This law assures the return of the seed that has been planted, but with the return of the seed alone nothing would have been gained by the process, and no food could be produced for man or beast.

No, there must be another law operating at the same time. We call it *the law of increasing returns*, for there is an increase in the amount produced. Nature gives back to the farmer the seed he planted in the ground, plus a margin of many times the amount of seed as his reward for having done more than he was temporarily paid for.

Everywhere and in everything may be seen the law of action and reaction in operation. Nature's budget is always balanced. Everything has its opposite equivalent in something else: positive and negative, in every unit of energy, day and night, hot and cold, summer and winter, good and bad, up and down, success and failure, sweet and sour, happiness and misery. The pendulum swings back the same distance that it swings forward.

So it is in human relationships and in the rendering of personal service. Whatsoever a man soweth, that shall he also reap. A man should remember that the kind of seed he sows is very important, because every seed of service yields a harvest after its own kind.

As I pointed out in the chapter on definiteness of purpose, man has absolute right of control over nothing else but the power of thought, which indicates that it must be his most valuable asset. Through the exercise of this divine gift, man has a voluntary avenue of approach to Infinite Intelligence, which means that he can place the forces of the entire universe behind his plans and behind his purpose.

After letting that tremendous idea sink in a while, I shall enumerate some of the more useful and important of the special benefits that are available to man if he will apply this principle. You might consider these items a sort of catalogue of reasons for going the extra mile. Here they are:

1. Going the extra mile places the law of increasing returns in back of your activities. This means that the quality and quantity of the services you give will come back to you greatly multiplied. You recall the story of the farmer and the grain of wheat that he plants as seed. If you render service that is worth $100, the chances are that eventually you will get back not only that $100, but ten times that amount if you render the service with the right mental attitude. Sometimes your increased return may not come back in dollars at all but in increased opportunity for you to get ahead through promotion or in making new friends.

   As you might have suspected, there is a converse to this law of going the extra mile. If you neglect to go the extra mile or don't even go the first mile, if you go after your service with a rather negative attitude in order to get an immediate compensation, the chances are that the law of diminishing returns will come into play, and you'll get back very much less than your grudging effort was worth, or possibly you will get back nothing at all.

2. The habit of doing more than you are paid for causes you to benefit by the law of compensation, through which no act or no deed will or can be expressed without an equivalent reaction after its own kind. To get appreciable results, this rule must be a habit applied at all times in all positive ways. You must ren-

der the greatest amount of service of which you are capable and render it in a friendly, positive manner. This principle of doing more than you are paid for operates for the benefit of the employer who applies it just as well as it does for the benefit of the employee. It would be just as unwise for an employer to withhold from an employee any portion of the wages he has justly earned as it would be for an employee to do less than he is paid to do.

Here is the fine point most people tend to overlook: until a man begins to render more service than he is paid for, he is already receiving full pay for what he does. The sad fact is that ninety-eight out of a hundred wage earners have no definite purpose greater than that of working for a daily wage. Therefore, no matter how much work they do or how well they do it, the wheel of fortune turns past them without giving them more than a bare living, because they neither expect nor demand more.

3. The habit of doing more than you are paid for will bring you to the favorable attention of those who have opportunities to offer. I have never yet known of any man promoting himself to a position of higher pay and greater responsibility without adopting and following this habit.

4. This habit enables you to become indispensable in many different human relationships and therefore to

command more than an average compensation for services. Although there may not be such a thing as an indispensable person per se, *indispensable* means someone or something you cannot get along very well without. Make yourself so useful that it would be extremely difficult, if not impossible, to replace you.

5. This habit leads to your mental growth and physical perfection in various forms of service, thereby developing greater ability and skill in your chosen vocation.

6. This habit protects you against the loss of employment and places you in a position to choose your own job and working conditions, in addition to attracting the self-promotional opportunities mentioned before.

7. Going the extra mile turns the spotlight on you, giving you the benefit of the law of contrast, which is very important in advertising yourself.

8. Doing more than you are immediately paid for leads to the development of a positive, pleasing attitude, which is among the most important traits of a pleasing personality. You can get almost anyone to act the way you wish towards you if you follow this law.

9. The habit of rendering more and better service than you are immediately compensated for develops personal initiative, without which no one may attain any position above mediocrity and without which no one

may acquire economic freedom. Personal initiative means doing what needs to be done without having somebody tell you to do it.

10. Going the extra mile gives you greater confidence in yourself and puts you on a better basis with your own conscience. Incidentally, if you have a full-length mirror in your home, it might be a good idea to walk right up to it and get acquainted with the guy in it. Talk to him about your plans and purposes. Enlist his cooperation. Explain to him how you have decided to adopt this master strategy of rendering extra service with the right mental attitude.

11. Going the extra mile aids in overcoming the destructive habit of procrastination. When you have the habit of going the extra mile, you are so eager to get things done that you learn to love the things you are doing and the person for whom you are doing it, and pretty soon Old Man Procrastination just dies of starvation.

12. Going the extra mile helps you develop definiteness of purpose, without which one cannot hope for success. It gives you definiteness of purpose because you are moving, speaking, and acting in response to a motive.

13. This habit gives you the right to ask for promotion and more pay. As long as you do only what you are paid to do, you have no logical reason for expecting

greater compensation; you must do what you are paid for in order to keep your job. But you have the privilege of rendering an overplus of service as the means of accumulating a reverse credit of goodwill, which entitles you to higher pay and a better position.

14. You may adopt and follow the habit of going the extra mile on your own initiative, without asking the permission of anyone to do so. I'd like to call your attention to the only formula in this entire philosophy: $Q + Q + MA = C$. *Quality of service* rendered plus *quantity of service* rendered plus the *mental attitude* in which it is rendered equals your *compensation* in the world and the amount of space you will occupy in the hearts of your fellow man. The word *compensation* here means all the things that come to you in life, whether it be money, joy, happiness, harmony in human relations, spiritual enlightenment, peace of mind, a positive mental attitude, the capacity for faith, the ability and desire to share blessings with others, a mind that is open and receptive to truth on all subjects, a sense of tolerance and fair play, or any other good, praiseworthy attitude or attribute you may seek.

Sometimes the law of compensation, which yields the return from the habit of going the extra mile, seems slow in operating. Sometimes the payoff comes from a source entirely removed from the one to whom the service has been rendered, but it will come as surely as night follows day.

Picture yourself as a strong, willing, dependable leader, a man amongst men, gladly doing more than your share, always eager to help. Now repeat these words at least three times a day:

→ *I willingly and gladly jump at any opportunity to serve people, even without compensation.*

→ *I willingly and gladly jump at any opportunity to serve people, even without compensation.*

→ *I willingly and gladly jump at any opportunity to serve people, even without compensation.*

→ *I willingly and gladly jump at any opportunity to serve people, even without compensation.*

→ *I willingly and gladly jump at any opportunity to serve people, even without compensation.*

→ *I willingly and gladly jump at any opportunity to serve people, even without compensation.*

→ *I willingly and gladly jump at any opportunity to serve people, even without compensation.*

→ *I willingly and gladly jump at any opportunity to serve people, even without compensation.*

→ *I willingly and gladly jump at any opportunity to serve people, even without compensation.*

→ *I willingly and gladly jump at any opportunity to serve people, even without compensation.*

6

Personal Initiative

"There are two types of men," said Andrew Carnegie, "who never amount to anything. One is the fellow who does not do what he is told to do. The other is the fellow who never does more than he is told to do. The man who gets ahead," he continued, "does what should be done without being told to do it, but he does not stop there. He goes the extra mile by doing a great deal more than is expected or demanded of him."

Personal initiative bears the same relationship to an individual that a self-starter bears to an automobile. It is the power that starts all action. Moreover, it is the power that inspires the completion of what one has begun.

There are many starters among men, but there are very few finishers. Personal initiative is the human dynamo that sets the faculty of the imagination into action by translating one's definite major purpose into its physical or financial equivalent. It is the quality that creates a major purpose as well as all minor purposes.

Personal initiative reveals favorable opportunities for self-advancement and inspires one to embrace and make the most of them. It reveals many faults and helps correct them. It gives one an unquenchable thirst for knowledge, new ideas, and better ways of doing things. It is the twin brother of the principle of going the extra mile. It inspired the writing of the Declaration of Independence and helped to translate that document into the freedom we enjoy today. It gave us the American system of free enterprise, a system whose most outstanding quality is that of inspiring all men with the right to act on their own personal initiative.

Personal initiative is a prominent quality of all successful leadership. It heads the list of qualities that a successful leader must possess. Personal initiative, to be effective as a quality of leadership, must be based upon a definite organized plan, inspired by a definite motive, and followed through to the end at which it is aimed.

An example of personal initiative in leadership is Henry J. Kaiser, who during World War II astounded the entire industrial world by his achievement of speed and efficiency in building ships. His achievements were all the more amazing because he had never built ships before. The secret of his success lies in his leadership ability.

Personal initiative is necessary for the application of the big four principles of personal achievement.

1. It inspires one to choose a definite major purpose and to follow through with a definite plan of action for attainment of that purpose.

2. It gives springs of action to the habit of going the extra mile.

3. It inspires the organization of a Master Mind alliance.

4. It clears the mind for guidance through applied faith.

These four principles would be of no value without personal initiative behind them.

The most common cause of failure, as I will state in the next chapter, is the habit of drifting through life without a definite major purpose. Individuals with personal initiative do not drift. They do not procrastinate. They do not complain of the lack of opportunity but move on their own responsibility and create opportunities for themselves. Examine the record of any successful man, and you will discover that he began with a definite major purpose and carried it through to completion on his own personal initiative.

Ponder over these facts, and you'll understand how and why the seventeen principles of this philosophy are related to one another like the links in a chain, and why success is attained by the application of a combination of the principles and not by any one of them singly.

A great philosopher said, "Everything a man needs comes to him by winding or straight paths, but not until he is ready to use it." Andrew Carnegie was ready for working capital when he decided to go into the steel business. He was ready because he conditioned his mind to use the capital profitably. He probably needed the money long before he received it, just as everyone needs money, but being in need is not the same as being ready to receive it. Mark well that difference, for it consists of the factors which enable one to switch over from the failure side of the river of life to the success side. Those factors consist of the proper use of some combination of the seventeen principles of this philosophy, the culmination depending upon the nature of one's need.

I repeat this truth at the risk of becoming monotonous because failure to understand it is fatal to success. I repeat it because it is the nature of man to search hither and yon for miraculous formulas for success, whereas the principles of success are simple and very understandable. And I repeat it because it is also the nature of man not to be impressed by any statement of truth when he first hears it.

This was demonstrated by the Master when he was approached by a rich man who was suffering from what he believed to be an incurable disease. The Master said, "Go wash seven times in the river Jordan, and you shall be cleansed." The rich man was not impressed. He was looking for a miraculous healing, something more impressive than the simple act of bathing himself in the dirty water of the river Jordan. But the Master knew that all healing begins by the conditioning of the mind to receive it, and this applies as much to the healing of the disease of poverty as to the healing of the physical body.

Everything a man needs comes to him when he is ready to use it. That principle was sound during the days of the Nazarene. It is no less sound today, for principles do not change from one generation to another. Moreover, principles of truth apply to all the circumstances of life, and their price consists of their understanding, application, and use—nothing more.

If you would be done with the negative side of the river of life, then make yourself free to switch over to the positive side. Move on your own personal initiative, for no one will move for you. Begin now, right where you stand. Adopt a definite major purpose. Lay out a plan for its attainment, and follow through with that plan. If the first plan does not work, change it for another, but you need not change your purpose. You may not have all the material things you need to carry out your purpose, but take hope from the fact that as you make the best possible use of such materials as you have, other and better materials will be made available to you if you are ready to receive and use them.

The mind that has been made ready to receive attracts what it needs as an electromagnet attracts steel filings. What greater opportunity, therefore, could one give to personal initiative than conditioning one's own mind to attract what one needs? The most difficult part of any task is making a start at performing it, but once a start has been made, the means of its performance presents itself. The truth of this has been proven by the fact that men with a definite major purpose are more successful than those without an objective. I have yet to find a man who carried a definite major purpose through to success who did not readily admit that his adoption of such a purpose was the major turning point in his entire life.

No one person can tell another what his definite major purpose in life should be, but any successful man will verify the fact that success is not possible without such a purpose. Adopt a definite major purpose. See how quickly the habit of moving on your own personal initiative will inspire you to action in carrying out the object of your purpose. Your imagination will become more alert, and it will reveal to you myriad opportunities related to your purpose. Opposition to your purpose will disappear. People will give you their friendly cooperation. Fear and doubt will disappear also. Somewhere along the way, you will meet your other self face-to-face, the self that can and will carry you over onto the successful side of the river of life.

From there on, the going will be easy and the way will be clear, for you will have adapted yourself to the great intangible forces of nature, which lead inevitably to the attainment of your chosen goal. Then you will wonder why you did not find that path sooner. You will also understand why success attracts more success, while a failure attracts only more failure.

All successful men follow the habit of acting on their own personal initiative, although some of them may apply this principle unconsciously. Most men who are failures drift through life aimlessly without plan or purpose, their efforts being dissipated by a lack of personal initiative in adopting a definite major purpose and carrying it through to completion.

Personal initiative is born out of motive. The Creator provided mankind with many ingenious methods of carrying out the divine plan for human advancement. One of these is planting enticing motives in a man's mind that influence him to do his best.

Love, sex, and the desire for economic security are the three most impelling of all the motives that inspire men to move on their personal initiative. Through the combined motives of love and sex the Creator has provided for the perpetuation of human life. They have been made so attractive that it is hardly within a man's choice to reject their influence.

The Creator has provided that life on earth shall continue according to his plans, no matter what man may think he wants or to what motives he may attribute the results of his personal initiative. Henry Ford may have believed that he was motivated by a desire for financial gain, or he may have believed he was motivated by his pride of achievement, through which he established a great industrial empire that gives employment directly and indirectly to many millions of people. Yet he may never have known—and it was not essential for him to know it—that through his efforts, millions of men are motivated to carry out the Creator's plans by developing their minds through personal initiative.

The human brain develops only by usage through personal initiative. This is a fact well known to every psychologist, but not everyone may recognize the possibility—nay, the probability—that back of all expression of all personal initiative is the Creator's plan to ensure man's mental and spiritual growth through his own endeavors. In the future we shall need to make the most of this new age of opportunity, in which men and women with creative vision, definiteness of purpose, and a motive will be inspired to move on their own personal initiative.

Let us not strangle American leadership and industry with the mistaken belief that impeding men and women of this kind is the way to help the weak and the poor, for it is obvious that without this leadership, we shall all be relegated to the class that, as a great philosopher once said, will always be with us. The best way to help the weak and the poor is to add incentive to the rich and the strong, like Edison and Ford, to move on their personal initiative. For obviously it is men like these who always have helped the weak and the poor to help themselves through profitable employment designed to inspire men to act on their own personal initiative.

The weak and the poor cannot be benefited by curtailing the rich and the strong or by depriving them of a motive to use their initiative. That would only have the effect of forcing all men to become weak and poor. Men who are wise will benefit by observing nature's plan with efficient mass-production methods, which have placed the necessities and the luxuries of life within the reach of the weak and the poor. The rich and the strong help by providing intelligent leadership, personal initiative, creative vision, imagination, and organized endeavor, through which the weak and the poor are provided with sources of income and opportunities to become rich and strong.

No one ever does anything voluntarily without an incentive. The three incentives of the highest order, as we have already stated, are love, sex, and the desire for financial gain. They are natural incentives, because they are inherent in every human being as gifts from the Creator. They must be a part of the divine plan of the Creator, or they would not have been planted in the minds of all normal human beings. The proper incentive has been responsible for the American way of life. Without it, the American way of life would now be the same as it was when we discovered this land of bounty.

True education does not come entirely from academic sources. Most practical education comes from human experience, from struggle, from trying and failing and then trying again. The word *educate* comes from the Latin word *educo*, meaning *to educe, to draw out, to develop from within*. The greatest inspiration to develop from within is that which provides a motive to create, build, accumulate property, and provide employment and opportunities for others. This type of motive has given us our best-educated men. If you do your work as I believe you can, the whole world will be richer because of your labor—not only in material things but in spiritual understanding, without which no form of riches can long endure.

See yourself vividly as a self-starter. You have a definite major purpose, you know where you are going, and you are on the move. Nothing can keep you from always acting towards your goals.

Now repeat these words:

→ *I persistently act and move towards my goals.*

→ *I persistently act and move towards my goals.*

→ *I persistently act and move towards my goals.*

→ *I persistently act and move towards my goals.*

→ *I persistently act and move towards my goals.*

→ *I persistently act and move towards my goals.*

→ *I persistently act and move towards my goals.*

→ *I persistently act and move towards my goals.*

→ *I persistently act and move towards my goals.*

→ *I persistently act and move towards my goals.*

7

Self-Discipline

In beginning this chapter, I am going to outline some definite benefits that you will receive from a mastery of the principle of self-discipline. If you will follow the instructions for using this principle, your imagination will become much more alert, your enthusiasm will become keener, your initiative will become more active, your self-reliance will be greater, the scope of your vision will be widened, and your problems will melt away as snowflakes in the noonday sun. You will look at the world through different eyes. Your personality will become more magnetic, and you will find people seeing you who had previously ignored or overlooked you. Your hopes and your ambitions will be stronger, and your faith will be more powerful.

That's a pretty good lineup of players for anybody's team, isn't it? I can promise you what I have just now because there is no single requirement for individual success as important as self-discipline.

Self-discipline means taking possession of your own mind. You have seen this theme repeatedly throughout this book, haven't you? Now we are at the point where you tie together the other principles we have studied and see the relationship between them as the links of a chain.

All the principles of this philosophy are for the express purpose of enabling you to develop control over yourself, which is the greatest of all essentials for success. If you could to do this with only one principle or one lesson, the others would, of course, be eliminated.

You are now studying the lesson that has been called the bottleneck through which all of your personal power for success must flow. The word *bottleneck*, as used here, indicates a controlled passageway that funnels all the rivulets of power that you have been mixing and blends them into a smooth-flowing river of great capacity.

Your mind is the think tank. That's right, a think tank—a vat or reservoir in which you have been creating and accumulating potential power. Now you're going to learn how to release that power in the precise quantities and in the specific directions that will best accomplish your purposes.

Through self-discipline, the power made available by each of the other principles of this philosophy becomes condensed and ready for practical application to your daily affairs. To use a rough analogy, you have been building an automobile to take you from where you are now to where you want to go. You have selected a definite major purpose based upon a compelling motive, which is your steering gear. You have adopted the master strategy of going the extra mile, which assures you of the cooperation of other people as a sort of transmission. You have actively and harmoniously associated yourself with certain other people through the Master Mind alliance, which gives you a kind of chassis. You have learned how to receive the power of Infinite Intelligence and focus it upon your objective by means of applied faith, which gives you a source of fuel energy or gasoline. You have the spark of a burning desire. Now you are learning how to coordinate all of these units into a smoothly functioning automobile with an engine of unlimited horsepower.

Self-discipline begins with the mastery of thought. If you do not control your thoughts, you cannot control your deeds; therefore, in its simplest form, self-discipline causes you to think first and act afterwards. Nearly everyone does exactly the reverse of this. Most people act first and think later, if and when they think at all.

Self-discipline gives you complete control over the fourteen major emotions, seven of which are positive, seven of which are negative. The seven positive emotions are love, sex, hope, faith, enthusiasm, romance, and desire. The seven negative emotions are fear, jealousy, hatred, revenge, greed, anger, and superstition. Now you can appreciate the value of eliminating or transmuting the seven negative emotions and exercising the seven positive emotions in the manner you desire.

Most people allow emotion to rule their lives; indeed it largely rules the world. But all of these emotions are states of mind and are therefore subject to your control and your direction. You can see instantly how dangerous the seven negative emotions can be if they are not mastered. The seven positive emotions can be destructive too if they are not organized and released under your complete conscious control.

A driving motive is the real starting point of all achievement. Everything that a man does centers around the major positive motive behind his definite major purpose in life. This motive must be so strong that it forces you to subordinate all of your thoughts and efforts to the attainment of that purpose.

Many people become confused between a real motive and a mere wish. Wishing will not bring success. If it did, everyone would be a howling success, because all people, of course, have wishes. They wish for everything on earth and even on the moon, but their wishes and their daydreams are as nothing until they are fanned into a white-hot flame of desire based upon a definite compelling motive. This must become the dominating influence of one's mind. It must assume obsessional proportions, which will induce action.

Self-discipline is a matter of adopting constructive habits, and self-discipline means the complete mastery of both your thought habits and your physical habits. I am about to give you one of the most important principles connected with self-discipline. It is so important that if you learn nothing more from this chapter, it will serve you well throughout the remainder of your life and help you to avoid most of the serious situations that face men and women who lack this key of understanding: *self-discipline calls for a balancing of the emotions of your heart with the reasoning faculty of your head.* You must learn to consult both your feelings and your reason in reaching decisions concerning great circumstances of your life.

Sometimes you will find it necessary to set aside your emotions entirely and to follow the dictates of your reason. At other times you will decide in favor of your emotions, modified by the advice of reason. Some men you probably know have so little control over their love emotions that they are like so much putty in the hands of a woman.

Some students have asked me if it would not be safer and wiser to control your life altogether with the reasoning faculty, leaving the emotions out of decisions and plans. I must say no to this question. It would be very unwise, if it were possible at all, because the emotions provide the driving power, the action force that enables a man to put the decisions of the head into operation. The emotions are the wellsprings of man's greatest power. If you destroy hope and faith, what would there be to live for? If you killed off enthusiasm or loyalty or the desire for achievement, you would have nothing left but reason, but what good would it be? The head would be there to direct, but it would not have anything to direct.

So far I have mentioned only the positive emotions, but the negative emotions can likewise be controlled and transmuted into a constructive driving force. Self-discipline can remove the stingers from these emotions and make them serve a useful purpose: as you know, sometimes fear and anger will inspire intense action. But all actions arising from the negative emotional impulses should have the modifying influence of the head so that they will be guided aright.

I want to explain another important idea concerning this balance between the head and the heart. This regards the willpower or the ego. I shall discuss this later in this chapter, but right here I want to point out that the willpower should be the final judge of any particular situation or circumstances and have the final say-so as to whether the reason or the emotions should be permitted to exert greater influence. Self-discipline should include an arrangement by which the ego or the willpower may throw its weight on the side of either the emotions or the reasoning faculties and may amplify the intensity with which either of these is expressed.

You see, both the head and the heart need a master, and they may find such a master in the willpower. The ego, acting through the will, sits as a presiding judge, but only for the person who has deliberately trained his ego for the job through self-discipline. In the absence of such self-discipline, the ego minds its own business and lets the head and the heart fight out their own battles as they please. In this case, the individual often gets badly hurt. We need self-discipline to control the emotions, especially in the case of four other items on the must list: appetite for food and drink, mental attitude, the use of time, and definiteness of purpose.

Now about this mental attitude: all through these lessons, I have repeatedly stressed the importance of a positive mental attitude as the only frame of mind in which you could have definiteness of purpose, induce anyone else to cooperate with you, or attract the power of Infinite Intelligence in applying your faith. A positive mental attitude is the first and the greatest of the twelve riches of life. Without it, it is impossible to enjoy any of the other twelve.

Indeed seven of the twelve great riches of life are directly traceable to self-discipline: positive mental attitude, harmony in human relationships, freedom from fear, the hope of achievement, the capacity for faith, an open mind on all subjects, and sound physical health. At this point it should not be necessary to dwell upon the importance of having a definite major purpose. You have seen how it is the beginning of all achievement when it is related to a strongly compelling motive.

If you haven't yet made up your mind what you want from life, now is the time to act. Go back and study the first chapter. Write out your chief aim and your plans for attaining it. This is the first step in self-discipline. You realize that even Infinite Intelligence, as all-powerful as it is, cannot help you if you do not make up your mind what you want and where you are going.

Sooner or later you will come to the point at which you will want to do something bigger and better than you have ever done before. When you arrive at that point, you are going to be discouraged by some of those around you who know you best and who will say that your plan is foolish or beyond your power to carry out. You will find a lot more people willing to tear you down with discouragement than those who will flatter you or build your ego. Of course, the best way to avoid such discouragement is to confide in no one but those who have a genuine sympathy with your cause and an understanding of your possibilities. Otherwise keep your plans to yourself. Let your actions speak. Adopt the motto *Deeds, not words.*

Take hold of the principles of this philosophy and apply them to yourself. The six divisions or departments of the mind that are subject to control by the individual are:

1. The ego. This is the seat of the willpower and acts as a supreme court, with the power to reverse, modify, change, or eliminate the entire work of all the other departments of the mind.

2. The emotions. Here is generated the driving force that sets one's thoughts and plans and purposes into action.

3. Reason. This is where one may weigh, estimate, and properly evaluate the products of the imagination and the emotions.

4. Imagination. This is where one may create ideas and plans and methods of attaining desired ends.

5. Conscience. This is where one may test the moral justice of one's thoughts and plans and purposes.

6. Memory. This serves as the keeper of records of all experiences and as a filing cabinet for all sense perceptions and the inspirations of Infinite Intelligence.

When these departments of the mind are coordinated and properly guided by self-discipline, they enable a person to negotiate his way through life with a minimum of opposition from others.

After studying this picture of the mind and realizing the tragedy of neglecting self-discipline, many students ask me the logical question: why has such a wonderful source of personal power been so overlooked? In all modesty, I must answer that this right of control over one's mind has been neglected because up to the time when Andrew Carnegie commissioned me to organize it, no one in modern times had provided the world with a practical philosophy that incorporated all the essentials of a well-managed life. In his dealings, the great builder of industry (and greater maker of men) learned of the great need for a philosophy such as this one. As I have said before, I am humbly grateful for having been the instrument by which this need has been fulfilled.

You are left without excuse for failure, because you have in your hands all the essential facts for attaining a high purpose. When a man coordinates the six departments of his own mind and brings them under his self-discipline, he finds himself in possession of more power than most men dream of.

Picture yourself as being strong and confident, yet calm and understanding. No matter what might happen to irritate or discourage you, you remain at all times thoughtful, purposeful, and resolute in the direction of your purpose. Now repeat these words:

→ *I think before I act.*
→ *I think before I act.*
→ *I think before I act.*
→ *I think before I act.*
→ *I think before I act.*
→ *I think before I act.*
→ *I think before I act.*
→ *I think before I act.*
→ *I think before I act.*
→ *I think before I act.*

8

Controlled Attention

Success in all the higher brackets of individual achievement is attained by the application of thought power properly organized and directed to definite ends. And power, whether it be thought power or physical power, is obtained by the concentration of energy. Concentration on one's major purpose projects a clear picture of that purpose upon the subconscious section of the mind and holds it there until it is taken over by the subconscious and acted upon. Thus prayer may be expressed as concentration on a definite objective and the strictest habits of self-discipline through these factors:

1. Definiteness of purpose, a starting point.

2. Imagination, which illuminates and mirrors the object of one's purpose in the mind so clearly that its nature cannot be mistaken.

3. The emotion of desire turned on until it attains the proportion of a burning desire that will not be denied fulfillment.

4. Faith in the attainment of the purpose, gained by the belief in its realization, which is so strong that one can see oneself already in possession of it.

5. Willpower applied continuously in support of faith.

The subconscious section of the mind picks up the picture thus conveyed to it and carries it out to its logical conclusion by whatever practical means may be available. Controlled attention leads to mastery in any type of human endeavor, because it enables one to focus the powers of his mind upon the attainment of a definite objective and to keep it so directed at will. Controlled attention is self-mastery of the highest order, because the man who controls his own mind may control everything else that gets in his way. Harriet Beecher Stowe was thinking of this sort of control when she said, "When you get into a tight place, and everything goes against you until it seems as though you could not hold on a minute longer, never give up then, for that is just the place and time that the tide will turn."

As a part of our description, we call your attention to a law of nature through which like attracts like. It is known as the *law of harmonious attraction*. Through it, forces and things that are suited to the needs of one another in the great scheme of life naturally tend to go together. We see this law in operation in connection with the vegetation that grows upon the soil of the earth. Through some strange and unknown process, this law manages to bring together the mineral and chemical elements of the soil and combine them with the units of energy of the air so as to produce everything that grows from the soil—the means by which all life on this earth is sustained.

When we consider relationships among men, we frequently find a situation in which the law of attraction is often disregarded, and unfriendly forces of thought energy often disrupt harmony. Sometimes this happens because of ignorance of the law of harmonious attraction, sometimes as a result of the deliberate substitution of negative thoughts, which are known to be destructive and opposed to the law of harmonious attraction. The person who has mastered the seventeen principles of this philosophy and has formed the habit of applying them in all of his relationships with other people benefits from the law of harmonious attraction by having conditioned his mind so it will attract to him only such people and material things as he desires. Moreover, he has eliminated from his own mind all conflicting emotions, such as fear, envy, greed, hatred, jealousy, and doubt, and has thus prepared his mind for applying the principle of controlled attention.

Great achievements come from minds that are at peace with themselves. Peace within one's mind is not a matter of luck, but a priceless possession, which can be attained only by self-discipline based upon controlled attention. Controlled attention is vastly different from casual interest. It is attained only by the strictest self-discipline, based upon definiteness of purpose.

One begins the act of controlled attention by knowing precisely what he desires to attain by it, then he proceeds by saturating his mind with that desire, giving it precedence over all other thoughts and recalling it to mind repeatedly by Master Mind discussions as well as by individual thinking. To use a familiar colloquialism, one controls the attention upon a given subject by thinking of it, talking of it, eating it, drinking it, sleeping it, and thus making it an obsession day and night. In this manner, the object of one's desires is forced upon the subconscious mind, that unusual faculty that works while one sleeps just as it does when one is awake. Eventually the subconscious mind takes over these obsessional desires and translates them into practical plans by which they may be obtained, handing the plans back to the conscious mind in the form of ideas that flash into the mind at unexpected moments.

Now I must reveal a truth that may shock you: every successful man I have ever known has developed his capacity for controlled attention to proportions that constituted self-hypnosis. As we have previously stated, one becomes influenced by and a part of the dominating circumstances of his daily environment. The medium by which this takes place is known as autosuggestion: suggestions one makes to oneself, either consciously or unconsciously. Autosuggestion records in the memory every thought one expresses, making it a part of his character, whether the thought is positive or negative. It records every word spoken within one's hearing and gives it a positive or a negative meaning according to one's reaction to it. Autosuggestion records a man's thought reactions to everything he sees or recognizes through any of the five physical senses, as well as the feel he picks up from his physical surroundings.

The objects on which a man deliberately concentrates his attention become the dominating influences of his environment. If his thoughts are fixed upon poverty or the physical signs of poverty, these influences are transferred to his subconscious mind through autosuggestion. Autosuggestion works in precisely the same manner when one's dominating thoughts are fixed through controlled attention upon opulence and economic security. Therefore when a man voluntarily fixes his attention upon a definite major purpose of a positive nature and, through his daily habits of thought, forces his mind to dwell on that subject, he conditions his subconscious mind to act on that purpose.

Controlled attention, when it is focused upon the object of one's definite major purpose, is a medium by which one makes positive application of the principle of autosuggestion. There are no other means by which this may be accomplished. The difference between controlled attention and attention which is not controlled is very great. It amounts to the difference between feeding the mind on thought material that will produce what one desires and allowing the mind by neglect to feed upon thought material which will produce what one does *not* desire. The mind never remains inactive, not even during sleep. It works continuously by reactions to the influences which reach it. Therefore the object of controlled attention is keeping the mind busy with thought material that may be helpful in attaining the object of one's desire.

Controlled attention may be likened to a gardener who keeps his fertile garden spot cleared of weeds so that he may make it yield edible foods. This simile is perfect, for it is well known that neglecting to keep the mind filled with positive thoughts results in its becoming filled with the weeds of the things one does not want.

An individual must either take charge of his mind and by controlled attention feed it with the type of food he wishes to reproduce, or he must pay the penalty of having his mind taken over by the negative influences of his own environment. There is no compromise between these two circumstances. One either takes possession of his own mind and directs it to the attainment of what he desires, or his mind takes possession of him and gives him whatever the circumstances of life hand out. The choice, however, is within the control of every human being. The fact that the power of thought is the only thing over which any human being has been given the right of complete control suggests the huge potentialities available through the exercise of this profound prerogative.

Once this principle of autosuggestion is understood, it will be easy to understand why the mind should be kept busy at all times in pursuit of a definite major purpose. That business keeps a mind out of mischief and forces it to work for and not against the individual. One noted psychologist described the working principle perfectly: "Autosuggestion is a tool with which we dig a mental path in the brain." Controlled attention is the hand that holds that tool. Habit is the map or blueprint which the mental path follows.

An idea or a desire to become transformed into action must be held in the conscious mind until habit gives it permanent form. From there on, autosuggestion does the rest by transferring the pattern to the subconscious mind, where it is taken over and automatically carried out to its logical conclusion by whatever practical means may be available.

Vividly and emotionally visualize yourself as already being the person you wish to be and already having the things that you desire. Hold that wonderful thought. Concentrate on the exhilarating feeling. Repeat these words several times a day:

→ *It is so easy and thrilling for me to concentrate all my thoughts on one thing: my goal.*

→ *It is so easy and thrilling for me to concentrate all my thoughts on one thing: my goal.*

→ *It is so easy and thrilling for me to concentrate all my thoughts on one thing: my goal.*

→ *It is so easy and thrilling for me to concentrate all my thoughts on one thing: my goal.*

→ *It is so easy and thrilling for me to concentrate all my thoughts on one thing: my goal.*

→ *It is so easy and thrilling for me to concentrate all my thoughts on one thing: my goal.*

→ *It is so easy and thrilling for me to concentrate all my thoughts on one thing: my goal.*

→ *It is so easy and thrilling for me to concentrate all my thoughts on one thing: my goal.*

→ *It is so easy and thrilling for me to concentrate all my thoughts on one thing: my goal.*

→ *It is so easy and thrilling for me to concentrate all my thoughts on one thing: my goal.*

9

Enthusiasm

Enthusiasm comes from the Greek words *en*, which means *in*, and *theos*, which means *god*. Enthusiasm comes from within, although it radiates outwardly in the expression of the voice and one's countenance. Enthusiasm is the utilization of the god within you and the ability to tap this great inner source of intelligence. It is no more or less than faith in action.

Inspired feeling, enthusiasm, is oftentimes confused with animated feeling. They are quite different, and we should understand this difference. Animated feeling can be quickly acquired at a pep rally or a sales meeting from external influence on the individual. You can easily acquire this feeling by singing, running around the house, jumping up and down, shouting, or through self-control. Likewise, animated feeling can be quickly lost. You can turn it on or shut it off like an electric light. Enthusiasm of the kind that we are speaking of here is hard to stop. It cannot be turned on or off at will. This faith in action will move a salesman over virtually any obstacle that he might encounter. With it, he can accomplish the impossible.

Enthusiasm puts into practice the premise that whatever the mind of man can conceive and believe, it can achieve. Enthusiasm causes one to glow. This radiant feeling is contagious. It will be grasped at once by your prospect and others who come into contact with you, and they will reflect it right back to you as their own feelings. Every successful salesman must have enthusiasm. Yes, every successful person must have enthusiasm.

As author Henry Chester said, "Enthusiasm is one of the greatest assets of man. It beats money and power and influence." Singlehanded, the enthusiast convinces and dominates where the wealth accumulated by a small army of workers would scarcely raise a tremor of interest. Enthusiasm tramples over prejudice and opposition, spurns inaction, storms the citadel of its object, and, like an avalanche, overwhelms and engulfs all obstacles. It is nothing less or more than faith in action.

Faith and initiative, rightly combined, remove mountainous barriers and achieve the unheard of and the miraculous. Set the germ of enthusiasm afloat in your plant, in your office, or on your farm. Carry it in your attitude and manner, and it spreads and influences every fiber of your industry before you realize it. It means increase in production and decrease in costs. It means joy and pleasure and satisfaction to your workers. It means life—real, virile. It means spontaneous bedrock results, the vital things that pay big dividends throughout life.

Enthusiasm bears the same relationship to a human being that fire bears to a steam boiler. It concentrates the powers of the mind and gives them the wings of action. Every philosopher and thinker has discovered that enthusiasm gives added meaning to words and changes the meaning of deeds. Some have discovered that it gives greater power to thought as well as to the spoken word. Enthusiasm is the offspring of motive. Give a man a burning desire to achieve a definite end and a definite motive back of that desire, and lo, the flame of enthusiasm begins to burn within him, and appropriate action follows immediately.

Inspirational author Orison Swett Marden said, "A man will remain a rag picker as long as he has only the vision of a rag picker." He might have said, "As long as he has only the enthusiasm of a rag picker," for it was this type of emotional feeling to which he had reference. "Our mental attitude, our heart's desire," he explained, "is our perpetual prayer, which nature answers. She takes it for granted that we desire what we are headed toward and she helps us to it." He might have expressed it as: "She takes it for granted that we desire what we are most enthusiastic about."

Another author, Lilian Whiting, caught the spirit and meaning of enthusiasm when she stated, "No one has success until he has the abounding life. This is made up of manifold activity of energy, enthusiasm, and gladness. It is to spring to meet the day with the thrill of being alive. It is to go forth to meet the morning in an ecstasy of joy. It is to realize the oneness of humanity in true spiritual sympathy."

Enthusiasm is a power because it is the instrument by which adversities and failures and temporary defeat may be transmuted into action backed by faith. This is perhaps the single most impressive truth that has been presented through the philosophy of individual achievement. It can be profoundly impressive to realize that sorrow and adversity can be transmuted into an impelling enthusiasm of sufficient force to enable one to surmount all difficulties.

Those who are interested in metaphysics know that material circumstances mean nothing to the person who understands how to turn on this enthusiasm at will, that material circumstances shape themselves to fit the state of one's mind as naturally as water runs down hills in response to the law of gravitation. The metaphysician knows that the death of a dear friend or loved one need not merely bring sorrow; it may serve as an inspiration to nobler efforts and deeper thinking through the transmutation of emotional feeling.

The power of thought is the one unsolved mystery of the world. We have found no evidence anywhere of the existence of energy except in one form. It is neither negative nor positive, but all energy can be applied in either a negative or a positive form.

Thought is an expression of energy. It is precisely as powerful when expressed in a negative form as it is when expressed in a positive form. Therefore the energy of thought, used to express the feeling of great sorrow, loss or disappointment, can be transmuted into positive expression and made to inspire noble endeavor. The transmutation hinges entirely upon the control of the emotions—hence the necessity of acquiring the habit of voluntary expression of enthusiasm.

There is but one kind of thought energy, but it can be given many kinds of expression, either negative or positive, or a combination of both. Reasoning on this simple premise, one can easily see that any negative emotion can be changed into a helpful positive feeling. In this possibility one may find the most profound application for enthusiasm.

The same energy that brings the pain of sorrow may be converted and made the joy of creative action in connection with one's definite major purpose or even some minor purpose. Here is where self-discipline comes to one's aid, for only the self-disciplined person can transmute sorrow into joy. Controlled enthusiasm steps up the vibration of thought and makes the faculty of the imagination more alert. It clears the mind of negative emotions by transmuting them into positive emotions, thereby preparing the way for the expression of faith. It aids the digestive organs in functioning normally. It gives a pleasing, convincing color to the tone of voice. It takes the drudgery out of labor. It adds to the attractiveness of the personality. It inspires self-confidence. It aids in the maintenance of sound physical health. It gives the necessary form to one's desires and influences the subconscious section of the mind to act with promptness on these desires. It generates enthusiasm on the part of others, for it is contagious as the measles or the whooping cough.

Enthusiasm converts an order taker into a first-class salesman. There has never been a salesman worthy of that title who could not turn on his enthusiasm at will and sustain it as long as he desired. Enthusiasm takes the dryness and boredom out of public speech by establishing harmony between the speaker and the audience; thus it is an indispensable quality for anyone whose occupation depends upon the spoken word for its success. The enthusiastic speaker takes control of the audience at will.

Enthusiasm gives brilliance to the spoken word and develops an alert memory. Being a sort of radiation of spirit, enthusiasm is closely related to—or at least attuned to—Infinite Intelligence, but far and away the most important functions of enthusiasm are these: it serves as the major factor in converting negative emotion into positive emotion, and it prepares the mind for the development and expression of faith. Compared with these, all other functions of enthusiasm are inconsequential. Enthusiasm is the action factor of thought. Where it is strong enough, it forces one into action appropriate to the motive that inspired it.

To develop the habit of enthusiasm, accurate thinking is the modus operandi for combining the emotions of the heart and the reasoning power of the head in whatever proportions each may demand. Enthusiasm, therefore, is an essential factor in effective thinking.

One may take certain steps that will lead to the development of controlled enthusiasm, and they are:

1. Adopt a definite major purpose and a definite plan for attaining it, and go to work carrying out the plan now right where you stand.

2. Back that purpose with an enthusiastic motive for its attainment. Let the desire become a burning desire. Fan it, coax it, and let it dominate your mind at all times. Take it to bed with you at night, and get up with it in the morning. Make it the basis of all your prayers.

3. Write out a clear statement of both your definite major purpose and the plan by which you hope to attain it, together with a statement of what you intend to give in return for its realization.

4. Follow the plan through with persistence based on all the enthusiasm you can generate, remembering that a weak plan persistently applied is better than a strong plan applied intermittently or without enthusiasm.

5. Keep as far away as possible from joy killers and confirmed pessimists. Their influence is deadly. Substitute in their place associates who are optimistic, and above all, do not mention your plans to anyone except those who are in full sympathy with you, such as the members of your Master Mind alliance.

6. If the nature of your definite major purpose requires it, ally yourself with others whose aid you require, following the instructions given in the chapter on the Master Mind.

7. If you are overtaken by temporary defeat, study your plans carefully, and if need be, change them, but do not change your major purpose because you have met with defeat.

8. Never let a day pass without devoting some time, even though it be ever so little, to carry out your plans. Remember you are developing the habit of enthusiasm, and habits call for repetition through physical action.

9. Autosuggestion is a powerful factor in developing any habit. Therefore keep yourself sold on the belief that you will obtain the object of your definite major purpose, no matter how far you may be from it.

Your own mental attitude will determine the action of your subconscious mind in fulfilling your purpose. Keep your mind positive at all times, remembering that enthusiasm thrives only on a positive mind. It will not mix with fear, envy, greed, jealousy, doubt, revenge, hatred, intolerance, or procrastination. Enthusiasm thrives on a positive action produced by a positive mind.

From here on out, you are on your own, but remember that every person lives in two worlds: (1) the world of his own mental attitude, which is greatly influenced by his associates and his physical surroundings, and (2) the physical world, in which he must struggle for a living. The circumstances of the physical world may be greatly shaped by the way one relates to his mental world. His mental world he may control. The physical world is beyond his control, except to the extent that he attracts the portion of it that harmonizes with his mental attitude.

Enthusiasm is a great leavening force in one's mental attitude and mental world. It gives power to one's purpose. It makes for harmony within one's mind. It helps to free the mind of negative influences. It wakes up the imagination and stirs one to action in shaping the circumstances of the physical world to one's needs. A man without enthusiasm or a definite major purpose resembles a locomotive with neither steam nor a track on which to run nor a destination towards which to travel.

General Douglas MacArthur had this to say about enthusiasm: "You are as young as your faith, as old as your doubt, as young as your self-confidence, as old as your fear, as young as your hope, as old as your despair. Years may wrinkle your skin, but to give up enthusiasm wrinkles your soul."

Now visualize yourself bursting with enthusiasm, power, and pride because of your sincere deep knowledge and conviction that you are successfully moving toward your goals. Repeat these words:

→ *I sizzle with enthusiasm and power.*

→ *I sizzle with enthusiasm and power.*

→ *I sizzle with enthusiasm and power.*

→ *I sizzle with enthusiasm and power.*

→ *I sizzle with enthusiasm and power.*

→ *I sizzle with enthusiasm and power.*

→ *I sizzle with enthusiasm and power.*

→ *I sizzle with enthusiasm and power.*

→ *I sizzle with enthusiasm and power.*

→ *I sizzle with enthusiasm and power.*

10

Creative Vision

Imagination is the key to all human achievements, the mainspring of all human endeavor, the secret door to the human soul. Imagination inspires endeavor in connection with material things and ideas associated with them.

Creative vision extends beyond the interest in material things: it judges the future by the past and concerns itself with the future more than with the past. Imagination is influenced and controlled by the powers of reason and experience. Creative vision pushes both of these aside and attains its ends by new ideas and methods. Imagination recognizes limitations, handicaps, and opposition. Creative vision rides over these as if they did not exist and arrives at its destination. Imagination is seated in the intellect of man. Creative vision has its base in the spirit of the universe, which expresses itself through the brain of man.

Note well these distinctions if you would know the difference between genius and mediocrity, for genius is the product of creative vision, while mediocrity is the product of the imagination (albeit one that often carries power and attains stupendous ends).

Our country needs creative vision now as it has never needed it before. Opportunities for expressing personal initiative were never as great as they are at this time. The nation has plenty of brawn and muscle, but it needs an expression of brainpower, and it needs it badly.

Two things are essential—more essential, perhaps, than all others—for unfolding and developing creative vision: one is a sincere willingness to work, and the other is a definite motive that is sufficient to inspire willingness to go the extra mile with a positive mental attitude. The great leaders of this and past generations began their careers in the humblest of capacities. By applying some combination of the seventeen principles of individual achievement, they promised themselves the goals they had set their hearts upon, but did not complain of the lack of opportunity.

Andrew Carnegie began as a bobbin boy in a textile mill at wages of 50 cents a day. Charles M. Schwab, who promoted himself to the position of Mr. Carnegie's first assistant, began as a stagecoach driver and later as a day laborer in the steel mills of Pennsylvania. Henry Ford began as an engineer for an electric light and power company. Thomas A. Edison began as a newsboy and later took up the work of telegraphy. The list could be extended to include practically every leader this nation has ever produced, each and every one of whom began his career under circumstances far less favorable than those enjoyed by the majority of the workers in industry today, and at far lower wages.

So it makes but little difference where a man begins; the important thing is, where is he going? Which does he watch the closest—the clock or the signs of an opportunity to make himself indispensable by the quality and the quantity of the service he renders? Every ambitious man should ask himself these questions, and he should be in a position to answer them.

The man who is blessed with creative vision knows where he is going. He knows what he desires of life. The man with creative vision knows that he can succeed only by helping others to succeed. The man with creative vision produces results instead of alibis. If he makes mistakes, as all men do, he is not afraid to accept the responsibility for them and never tries to shift that responsibility to another man. He makes decisions quickly but changes them just as readily when he discovers that he has made the wrong decision. He has no fear of others, either those of higher rank or lower rank than himself, for he is at peace with his own conscience, fair with his fellow men, and honest with himself.

Creative vision is not a miraculous quality with which one is gifted or not gifted at birth. It may be developed. If it were not so, this chapter would be useless. Personal achievement, power, fame, and riches—each has a definite price, and the man with creative vision not only knows the price but is willing to pay it. Moreover, the man with creative vision understands the benefits of sharing his blessings, experience, and opportunities with others, for he recognizes that only by this method can he attain and enjoy enduring prosperity, happiness, and the respect of others.

The products of imagination and creative vision are vastly different. The history of nations from the days of the fall of the Roman Empire to the present clearly indicates that nations begin their decline when creative vision ceases to be the dominating force in their leaders. We still have many men with creative vision in the United States, but most of them are engaged in business and industrial pursuits. They have given us the greatest system of free enterprise the world has ever known, but we need great statesmen as well if our form of government and our system of free enterprise are to survive. It is true, as the great philosopher has stated, that man shall not live by bread alone. America needs creative vision in every field of endeavor, and the man or woman who masters this philosophy and learns to apply it will be sure to supply a generous portion of this vision, for which equally generous rewards await them.

Men of vision have provided us with the means by which we may press a button at sundown and lo, the sun shines again. They have given us machines that record and reproduce the sound of the human voice by the mere pressing of another button. They have harnessed the boundless ether and made it serve as a means of quick communication between the peoples of all the world. By the same device, they have provided every home in our land, from the humblest to the greatest, with the news of the world as fast as it occurs as well as the finest musical programs, all without cost. They have ushered in the great steel age, the automobile age, the electric age, the skyscraper age, the airplane age, and the far-flung industrial age, which have made our country the richest and most envied in the world. They have given us the finest system of public schools that civilization has ever known and a system of public libraries through which we may avail ourselves, without cost, of all the accumulated knowledge of mankind. And men of vision laid the foundation for all of these blessings by placing their names to the most famous document that was ever produced by man—the Declaration of Independence—although they well knew that they were signing a document that might well become either their death warrant or a license for liberty for all the people of the United States. Men of vision inserted a piece of glass in a metal tube, turned it toward the heavens, and revealed the presence of worlds that the human eye had never seen before.

Power is essential for enduring success—not the type of power that is based upon force and coercion and fear, but the type that is produced by creative vision. This truth applies to both individuals and groups. Creative vision may be an inborn quality of the mind, or it may be an acquired quality, for it may be developed by the free and fearless use of the faculty of imagination.

There are two types of imagination. The first is *synthetic imagination*, which combines recognized ideas, concepts, plans, or facts and arranges them in a new order or put them to a new use. Genuinely new ideas are rarely revealed, and they are never revealed except to those with creative vision. Nearly every fact or idea known to or used by modern civilization is but a combination of something old that has been rearranged in a new combination.

The other type of imagination is *creative imagination*, which has its base in the subconscious section of the mind and serves as the medium by which new facts or ideas are revealed through the sixth sense. Psychologists know that any idea, plan, or purpose that is brought into the conscious mind repeatedly and supported by emotion is automatically picked up by the subconscious section of the mind and carried out to its logical conclusion by means of whatever practical media are at hand.

Creative vision is closely related to faith, and those who have demonstrated the greatest amount of creative vision have been individuals with a great capacity for faith. This is understandable when we recognize that faith is the means of approach to Infinite Intelligence, the source of all knowledge and all facts both great and small.

Creative vision expressed by men and women who have been unafraid of criticism has been responsible for civilization as we know it. It has been responsible for the revelations of scientific inventions, because it inspires men to pioneer and experiment with new ideas in every field of endeavor. It is forever on the lookout for better ways of doing human labor and supplying human needs. Creative vision belongs only to men and women who follow the habit of going the extra mile, for it recognizes no such thing as regular working hours, it is not concerned with monetary compensation, and its highest aim is to do the impossible. When a man's imagination goes to work, his hands follow suit, for imagination inspires one with the enthusiasm that makes all work a labor of love.

You may need creative vision as a guiding force in your life. If so, you might begin developing it by getting on better terms with your own conscience, inspiring yourself with greater self-reliance, providing yourself with a definite major purpose in life, keeping your mind so busy with your major purpose that you have no time left for fear and doubt, and finding out who you are, what you want from life, and what you have to give in return.

Lastly, you might adopt the habit of the silent hour, when you are still and listen for the voice that speaks from within, thus discovering the greatest of all powers—creative vision—the one power that can shift one from the failure side of the river of life over to the success side. During your silent hour, you will be alone with yourself and your God. This is one hour you cannot share with any other. You must go into the silence alone, of your own free will and accord. After you get there, you must speak for yourself. No one can speak for you, and nothing will happen save what you have inspired by your own initiative. Nothing of great importance may happen to you outside of your silent hour, except what you inspire by your own personal initiative, and creative vision inspires the development of personal initiative.

Labor without imagination has a fixed market price for each class of work. When mixed with imagination, the price of labor may be without a limit.

Picture yourself as an indomitable power filled with positive thinking, a positive mental attitude, and faith that you are achieving your goals. You are relaxed and confident. Three times a day, get alone, get quiet, completely relaxed, and then think and repeat:

- ↣ *Ideas are now coming to me that will help me achieve my goal; I thankfully and gratefully accept them.*

- ↣ *Ideas are now coming to me that will help me achieve my goal; I thankfully and gratefully accept them.*

- ↣ *Ideas are now coming to me that will help me achieve my goal; I thankfully and gratefully accept them.*

- ↣ *Ideas are now coming to me that will help me achieve my goal; I thankfully and gratefully accept them.*

- ↣ *Ideas are now coming to me that will help me achieve my goal; I thankfully and gratefully accept them.*

- ↣ *Ideas are now coming to me that will help me achieve my goal; I thankfully and gratefully accept them.*

- ↣ *Ideas are now coming to me that will help me achieve my goal; I thankfully and gratefully accept them.*

- ↣ *Ideas are now coming to me that will help me achieve my goal; I thankfully and gratefully accept them.*

- ↣ *Ideas are now coming to me that will help me achieve my goal; I thankfully and gratefully accept them.*

- ↣ *Ideas are now coming to me that will help me achieve my goal; I thankfully and gratefully accept them.*

- ↣ *Ideas are now coming to me that will help me achieve my goal; I thankfully and gratefully accept them.*

11

Learning from Adversity and Defeat

The central theme of this principle may be stated in one simple sentence: *every adversity carries with it the seed of an equivalent or a greater benefit.*

At first this statement may be difficult to accept, but let us examine the evidence of its truth before we try to pass judgment on its soundness. Everyone knows that failure and physical pain are part of nature's common language, in which she speaks to every living creature. This language brings human beings into the spirit of humility so they may acquire wisdom and understanding.

The turning point at which one begins to attain success in the higher brackets of achievement is usually marked by some outstanding defeat or failure. Recognition of this fact may in itself mark the most important turning point of one's life, because it may lead to the astounding discovery that temporary defeat need not be accepted as failure, that most so-called failures represent only temporary defeat, which may prove to be a blessing in disguise.

Although the circumstances of life are such that everyone must undergo a certain amount of temporary defeat, one may find hope in the knowledge that every such defeat carries within it the seed of an equivalent benefit. This knowledge enables one to modify one's mental reactions instead of accepting defeat as permanent failure.

Defeat is never the same as failure unless and until it has been accepted as such. "Our strength," said Emerson, "grows out of our weakness. Not until we are pricked and stung and sorely shot at does it awaken the indignation which arms itself with secret forces. A great man is always willing to be little. Whilst he sits on the cushion of advantages he goes to sleep. When he is pushed, tormented, defeated, he has a chance to learn something. He has been put on his wits, on his manhood. He has gained facts, learns his ignorance, is cured of the insanity of conceit. He has got moderation and real skill."

There you have the major benefits of defeat. They have been stated by a great thinker in terms anyone may understand and whose soundness anyone may test by one's own experience. Defeat, of course, does not promise the full-blown flower of benefit—only the seed from which some benefit equivalent in scope to the defeat may be attained. The seed must be recognized; it must be germinated, nurtured, and cultivated by definiteness of purpose. The seed will not germinate except by these means, for here, as everywhere, nature looks with disfavor on the endeavor to obtain something for nothing.

Yes, there is a wheel on which the affairs of men revolve, and although it prevents anyone from always being fortunate, it also prevents anyone from always being unfortunate. This wheel may be likened to a great river, one half of which flows in one direction and carries all who enter it to inevitable success, while the other half flows in the opposite direction and as definitely carries all who enter it to failure and defeat. The river is not imaginary but real. It might well be called the river of life. It exists in the power of human thought, dwells in the mind of man, and is the one and only power over which human beings have been provided with full and complete right of unchallenged and unchallengeable control.

The success side of the river of life is attainable through definiteness, applied faith, the Master Mind, and a willingness to go the extra mile—the big four of the seventeen principles of individual achievement. Banks may fail and sweep away one's material fortune, friends and loved ones may pass away, ill-health may make its appearance, cheaters may steal, and liars may destroy reputation and deprive one of favorable opportunities. Unfavorable seasons may destroy the fruits of one's labor through drought or tornado; business depressions may deprive one of honest employment. All of these and many more unavoidable circumstances—which are clearly beyond one's immediate control—may and often do overtake individuals. Yet each and every one of them carries with it the seed of an equivalent benefit.

Near Fort Atkinson, Wisconsin, a farmer by the name of Milo C. Jones operated a small farm. Although his physical health was good, he seemed unable to make his farm yield more than the bare necessities of life. Late in life, he was overtaken by an unavoidable circumstance that most men would accept as failure: he was stricken by double paralysis and was put to bed by relatives, who believed him to be a hopeless invalid. For weeks he remained in bed, unable to move a single muscle. All he had left was his mind, the one great power he had drawn upon so rarely because he had earned his living by the use of his brawn. Out of sheer necessity, he discovered that mind and began to draw upon it. Almost immediately he discovered a seed of an equivalent benefit that was destined to compensate him for his misfortune. He recognized the seed, germinated it by applying the Master Mind principle, and put it to use. The seed consisted of a single idea—an idea, let us remember—that he probably would never have discovered had he not been driven to it by temporary defeat.

After the idea had been thoroughly organized in his mind, Jones called members of his family and revealed it to them. "I can no longer work with my hands," he began, "so I have decided to work with my mind. The rest of you will have to take the place of my hands. I wish you to plant every acre of our farm you can spare in corn, then start raising pigs with that corn. Slaughter the pigs while they are young and tender, then convert them into sausage. Let us call it 'Little Pig Sausage.' We will sell it directly to the retail stores all over the country."

The family went to work as directed. In a few years, the trade name of Little Pig Sausage became a household byword throughout the nation, and the Jones family became far richer than they had ever dreamed. Milo C. Jones lived to see himself a multimillionaire, and all of his fortune was earned on the same farm that, previous to his misfortune, had yielded him but a scant living. He had switched over from the failure side of the river of life to the success side of the stream.

A prolonged illness often forces one to stop, look, listen, and think. Thus one may approach an understanding of the still, small voice that speaks from within and take inventory of the causes that have led to defeat and failure in the past. The death of a dear friend, spouse, brother, or lover, which seemed nothing but privation, later assumes the aspect of a guide or genius. It commonly revolutionizes our way of life, terminates an epoch of infancy or youth that was waiting to be closed, breaks up an unwanted occupation or a household or style of living, or allows the formation of new ones more friendly to the growth of character. It permits or constrains the formation of new acquaintances and the reception of new influences that prove to be of first importance. The man or woman who would have remained a sunny garden flower with no room for its roots and too much sunshine for its head is, by the falling of the walls and the neglect of the gardener, made the banyan of the forest, yielding shade and fruit to wide neighborhoods of men. Thus speaks the philosopher, who determines causes by analyzing their effects, for he discovers that every human experience, whether it be pleasant or unpleasant, has within it the seed of some good.

Abraham Lincoln, whom many believe to have been our greatest American citizen, was born in poverty and illiteracy. The circumstances of his birth and early life were beyond his control. As a young man, he aspired to be a merchant but adversity overtook him and so did the sheriff. He turned to the study of law, but his lack of skill was such that he found but few clients. He joined the army, was inducted as a captain, and was sent to fight Indians in the West. When he returned, he had been demoted to the status of a private, and some believe he was lucky not to have been court-martialed. Everything he touched turned to failure. At long last, he was overtaken by the greatest misfortune of his meteoric life when Anne Rutledge, the woman he truly loved, passed away. That adversity reached down deeply into the great soul of Abraham Lincoln, the nobody from nowhere, awakened the secret forces within that soul, and brought forth a great American emancipator. Verily there is no such thing as failure, save only the circumstance that is accepted as such.

When you have been struck down by circumstances that you regard as failure, remember that you may be face-to-face with the needed turning point in your life, from which you may change your course, get on a new road, and acquire new courage, new vision, and a new will to win.

The compensating benefits of failure and defeat often cannot be seen or recognized as benefits until one looks backward at the experiences after a sufficient lapse of time to provide a healing of the wounds. A great philosopher has truly said, "God never takes anything away from anyone without replacing it with something better." The history of mankind proves the soundness of this statement, and the evolutionary forces that have lifted civilization upward and onward prove it. Time eventually corrects all evils and rights all wrongs for those who recognize that adversity doth often teach men lessons they would learn only by adversity.

Test this principle of learning from defeat and benefiting by adversity by any method the imagination can conceive. Measure it by all the evidence that may be at hand, and it will remain unshaken as a sound principle as inexorable as the laws that give orderliness to the universe.

Despite the soundness of this principle, no one courts adversity or failure; most people will desire to avoid failure wherever they can anticipate it. One may not always control the outward effects of defeat when it involves the loss of material things or damages other people, but one may control one's own reactions to the experience and profit by it.

Defeat may supplant vanity and arrogance with humility of heart, paving the way for the formation of more harmonious human relationships. Defeat may cause one to acquire the habit of taking self-inventory in order to uncover the weakness that brought on the defeat. Defeat may lead to the development of a stronger willpower, provided one accepts it as a challenge to greater effort and not as a signal to stop trying. This, perhaps, is the greatest potential benefit of all forms of defeat, because the seed of an equivalent benefit, which exists in the circumstances of the defeat, abides entirely in one's mental attitude or one's reaction toward it. It is therefore under his control.

Defeat may break up undesirable relationships with others and thus prepare the way for the formation of more beneficial relationships. Very few people are fortunate enough to be able to go through life without forming social, business, professional, or occupational relationships that are detrimental to their own interests but which can be broken by nothing less than some form of defeat.

Defeat such as the loss of loved ones through death, the breaking up of a love affair, or the destruction of a deep friendship may lead one into the deeper wells of sorrow, where he may discover spiritual forces he had not previously recognized. These experiences force one to seek consolation from within one's own soul. In the search, one sometimes finds the door that leads to a huge reservoir of a hidden power that would never have been revealed except through defeat. This type of defeat often diverts one's attention and activities from the material values of life to the spiritual values. It may be assumed, therefore, that the Creator gave man a deep capacity for sorrow in order that it might influence him to avail himself of the spiritual forces of his own soul.

The person who can go through a defeat that crushes the finer emotions and still avoid having his inner soul smothered by the experience may become a master in his chosen field. From such experiences have developed many of the world's great musicians, poets, artists, builders of empires, and literary geniuses. The truly great artists in these and other fields of endeavor attained greatness through some tragedy that introduced them to the hidden forces of their own being. When one finds these forces, which reveal themselves from within, he may discover that they can be transmuted into any desired form of creative effort instead of serving merely to heal the wounds of the heart. These forces may lead to great heights of individual achievement in a spirit of humility, which alone can make one truly great. Success without humility of the heart is apt to prove only temporary and unsatisfying.

If we examine the records of men and women in the humbler walks of life, we shall be convinced that those who attain success are those who have accepted defeat as nothing but an urge to greater and better-planned action. We shall find too that individual success is usually in exact proportion to the scope of the defeat the individual has experienced and mastered. The man who fails and still fights on usually uncovers a source of creative vision that enables him to convert temporary defeat into permanent success. Therein lies the major benefit of defeat. Defeat, as one man stated it, forces a man to decide whether he is a man or a mouse.

Defeat often serves to relieve a man of his conceit, but let no one be deceived about the difference between conceit and self-reliance based upon an honest inventory of one's character. The man who quits when defeat overtakes him thereby indicates that he mistook his conceit for self-reliance. If a man has genuine self-reliance, he has also sound character, for one evolves from the other, and sound character does not yield to defeat without a fight. The man with a definite major purpose, faith, and determination may, because of circumstances beyond his control, be swept occasionally from the success side of this great river to the failure side, but he will not long remain there, because his mental reactions to his defeat will be sufficiently strong to carry him back to the success side, where he rightfully belongs.

Realize that failure or defeat are only temporary—nature's way of bringing out humility and wisdom and understanding. Realize too that with every adversity there is the seed of an equivalent or greater benefit. Now repeat:

→ *In any adversity, I recognize no failure, no defeat. I look instead for the seed of an equivalent benefit, and I fight on persistently toward my goal, thankful for the lesson I learned.*

→ *In any adversity, I recognize no failure, no defeat. I look instead for the seed of an equivalent benefit, and I fight on persistently toward my goal, thankful for the lesson I learned.*

→ *In any adversity, I recognize no failure, no defeat. I look instead for the seed of an equivalent benefit, and I fight on persistently toward my goal, thankful for the lesson I learned.*

➔ *In any adversity, I recognize no failure, no defeat. I look instead for the seed of an equivalent benefit, and I fight on persistently toward my goal, thankful for the lesson I learned.*

➔ *In any adversity, I recognize no failure, no defeat. I look instead for the seed of an equivalent benefit, and I fight on persistently toward my goal, thankful for the lesson I learned.*

➔ *In any adversity, I recognize no failure, no defeat. I look instead for the seed of an equivalent benefit, and I fight on persistently toward my goal, thankful for the lesson I learned.*

➔ *In any adversity, I recognize no failure, no defeat. I look instead for the seed of an equivalent benefit, and I fight on persistently toward my goal, thankful for the lesson I learned.*

➔ *In any adversity, I recognize no failure, no defeat. I look instead for the seed of an equivalent benefit, and I fight on persistently toward my goal, thankful for the lesson I learned.*

➔ *In any adversity, I recognize no failure, no defeat. I look instead for the seed of an equivalent benefit, and I fight on persistently toward my goal, thankful for the lesson I learned.*

➔ *In any adversity, I recognize no failure, no defeat. I look instead for the seed of an equivalent benefit, and I fight on persistently toward my goal, thankful for the lesson I learned.*

12

Budgeting Time and Money

Brace yourself, because the time has come for some very plain talk about you and your future. We have come a long way on the road that leads to happiness, and we have reached the twelfth gate through which we shall have to pass. It is headed, "Budgeting of Time and Money." After we pass through this gate, we shall know how to make the most of our time and how to acquire money and make it serve a noble purpose.

Let us tarry by the wayside as we pass through gate number twelve, while we ponder over the knowledge we have gained as we progressed through the preceding gates. If we have been observing students, we now have more useful knowledge than most college graduates acquire during four to six years of college training, but it is not theoretical knowledge, because it was provided by men of practical experience, who attained it through trial and error from their own rich experience. All we have learned from the experiences of these men is very important, but we now come to the place where we must forget other men and their achievements and direct our attention to you and your future.

This is your personal inventory time. You are face-to-face with some facts that may not be pleasant, but let us face these facts courageously. Yes, we all have alibis, but remember that alibis will not bring you what you desire in life. Ask yourself this question: are you a success or a failure? If you're a failure, no amount of explanation will change the results, for the one thing the world will never forgive is failure. The world wants successes, it worships successes, but it has no time for failures. The only way a man may explain away his failure is by trimming his sails through self-discipline so that the circumstances of his life will lead him to success.

It is a great day in a man's life when he sits down quietly and has a heart-to-heart talk with himself, because he is sure to make discoveries about himself that will be helpful, although they may give him a shake. Nothing is ever accomplished by merely wishing, hoping, or daydreaming. Earnest self-analysis helps one to rise above these. No one can get something for nothing, although many have tried. Everything worth having has a definite price, and that price must be paid. The circumstances of one's life makes this essential.

Success does not require a great amount of knowledge about anything, but it does call for the persistent use of whatever knowledge one may have. Successful men know themselves not as they think they are, but as their habits have made them; therefore you are requested to take inventory of yourself so that you may discover where and how you are using your time. How are you using your time? How much of it are you wasting, and how are you wasting it? What are you going to do to stop this waste? These questions are important and claim earnest attention.

Broadly speaking, there are two classes of people: the drifters and the nondrifters. A nondrifter is a person who has a definite major purpose and a definite plan for its attainment and is busily engaged in carrying out that plan. He thinks his own thoughts and assumes full responsibility for them, whether they are right or wrong. A drifter does no real thinking, but accepts the thoughts, ideas, and opinions of others and acts upon them as if they were his own. The drifter follows the line of least resistance on all occasions and repeats his mistakes over and over, while the nondrifter takes pride in blazing new trails, mastering new hazards, and learning from his mistakes. A nondrifter expresses action through definiteness of purpose and follows the habit of going the extra mile in carrying out his purpose. He moves on his own personal initiative without pressure from others. He controls all of his habits, of thought and of action, through the strictest self-discipline. He maintains a positive mental attitude and thinks in terms of what he desires most, not of what he does not desire. He supports his actions with applied faith. He surrounds himself with a Master Mind group in order to have the cooperation of others whose knowledge and experience he needs to carry out his purpose. He recognizes his weaknesses and finds ways and means of bridging them. He takes personal inventory of himself as regularly as a first-class merchant takes inventory of his stock.

I wish now to reveal the circumstances under which the drifter fails to make effective use of his time. This outline should be used as a measuring stick by those who wish to take personal inventory of themselves, for it will reveal the ten major sources of drifting.

1. **Occupation**. A man's occupation is the source of his economic opportunity. The average man devotes five days out of every seven to his occupation. The majority of people, the drifters, never concern themselves over the selection of an occupation that is suited to their education or to their mental and spiritual temperaments. Accurate analysis of the nondrifter shows clearly that he is engaged in an occupation of his own

choice; therefore he is engaged in a work that truly is a labor of love, one of the twelve riches of life, into which he willingly projects his creative ability, his enthusiasm, his hopes and his aims.

2. **Habits of thought**. The drifter makes no attempt to discipline or control his thoughts and never learns the difference between negative thoughts and positive thoughts. He allows his mind to be occupied with any stray thought that may float into it. People who drift in connection with their thought habits are sure to drift on other subjects as well. A positive mental attitude is the first and the most important of the twelve riches of life, and it cannot be attained by the drifter. It *can* be attained by a scrupulous regard for time through self-discipline. No amount of time devoted to one's occupation can compensate for the benefits of a positive mental attitude, because this is the power that makes the use of time effective and productive.

3. **Business, professional, and personal relationships**. Success in the higher brackets of achievement is attained through friendly cooperation in association with people who do not drift. Harmony in human relationships leads to confidence, and confidence leads to friendly cooperation. Friction, conflict, and misunderstanding interrupt friendly relationships and waste time in almost every walk of life. It is well

to remember also that successful men have no time for the drifter, who has so little regard for his own time that he is willing to waste it in useless argument over trivialities.

4. **Habits of health**. Here the habit of drifting attains its most tragic proportions, for it is a recognized fact that average man pays more attention to the care of his automobile than to the care of his own health. The subject of health cannot be emphasized too greatly. The drifter worries, frets, nags, complains, and fears the imaginary dangers that he believes may overtake him, until the chemist within his body goes on a sit-down strike and ceases to keep a balance between the elements the body needs to maintain sound health and those that lead to illness. The drifter is a queer combination of indifference, indecision, confusion, and irregularity of habits of both thought and deed.

5. **Religion**. Religions are good because they inspire the individual to recognize that he has spiritual qualities available for his every need. But here we find procrastination no less evident than it is in connection with the habits which lead to sound physical health. To most people, religion is something to be embraced and believed in for the sake of decency, but not necessarily to be lived. To the majority of those who embrace it, religion is a theory more than a practice.

6. **Use of spare time**. Spare time may be defined as the portion of one's time that is not devoted to one's occupation. The use one makes of spare time is an accurate means of foretelling his future, for this is the period when his thoughts may be controlled and directed to any desired end. For the person who works for others, spare time is a promotion, because it is when he may prepare for greater responsibilities. The drifter usually is as careless with his time as with his money. He fails to recognize that time is the same as money, and he spends both with reckless disregard for their value.

7. **The habit of unbudgeted spending**. Here is a time killer of the first order. It not only kills time but leads to penury and want. Every successful business and industry is operated on a strict system of budget control, which gives an accounting of both time and money expenditures. Every successful individual must manage his life on the same basis. The popular American system of installment buying is a great convenience to millions of people, but it can be, and often is, overdone for lack of a practical system of budget spending.

8. **Family relationships**. The amount of time wasted through maladjustment in family relationships is appalling. The burden of the sins of this waste rests upon the shoulders of parents, for they usually set

the example for the entire family. The family circle is the place where character is formed, and it should be guarded with profound regard for its responsibilities. The head of the family cannot succeed in his chosen occupation unless he has the peace of mind that grows out of harmony in his home. Harmony is the result of careful planning, budgeting income and expenditures, and fixing of family responsibilities for every member of the family.

9. **You and your job**. The time wasted by men and women who work for wages is sufficient in the aggregate for building another industrial system twice the size of the great American system of industry. It is sufficient also to provide every worker with an additional income as great or greater than he now receives for the kind of service rendered by the average worker.

10. **Accurate thinking**. Most people drift into the habit of guessing instead of gathering, organizing, and classifying facts upon which to build plans and reach decisions. The drifter has an opinion on almost every subject, but he seldom takes the time to procure accurate information concerning any subject. The nondrifter has no opinion except those created from carefully gathered facts or reasonable hypotheses of facts. He is careful not to express an opinion that is not based upon known facts.

The habit of saving money should be practiced by setting aside a definite percentage of all income. When the savings fund is large enough, it should be put into some kind of safe investment, where it will begin to multiply itself. It should not be used for current expenses, nor should it be used for emergencies as long as they can be handled by other means.

Time is a master worker, which heals the wounds of defeat and disappointment, rights all wrongs, and turns all mistakes into capital, but it favors only those who kill off procrastination and move toward the attainment of some preconceived objective with definiteness of purpose. Second by second, as the clock ticks off the distance, time is running a race with every human being. Delay means defeat, because no man may ever make up a single second of lost time. Move with decision and promptness, and time will favor you. If you hesitate or stand still, time will wipe you off the board. The only way you can save time is to spend it with wisdom.

Now picture yourself as a master of both time and money. You have no time for time wasters or money wasters. Repeat:

→ *I spend my time and money wisely and cautiously.*

→ *I spend my time and money wisely and cautiously.*

→ *I spend my time and money wisely and cautiously.*

→ *I spend my time and money wisely and cautiously.*

→ *I spend my time and money wisely and cautiously.*

→ *I spend my time and money wisely and cautiously.*

→ *I spend my time and money wisely and cautiously.*

→ *I spend my time and money wisely and cautiously.*

→ *I spend my time and money wisely and cautiously.*

→ *I spend my time and money wisely and cautiously.*

13

A Positive Mental Attitude

At birth, each human being brings along the equivalent of two sealed envelopes. They contain a list of the riches he may enjoy by taking possession of his own mind and using it to attain the things he desires in life, and a list of the penalties that nature will exact from him if he neglects to recognize and use his mind power.

Nature discourages and penalizes two things: (1) a vacuum, emptiness; (2) idleness, lack of action. You either use your brain for controlled thinking in connection with things you want, or nature steps in and uses it to grow you a marvelous crop of negative circumstances that you do not want. You have a choice in this connection. You can take possession of your thought power, or you can let it be influenced by all the stray winds of chance and circumstance you do not desire.

Out of this great truth has grown the saying, "Success attracts more success while failure attracts more failure." You must have observed this truth many times, although you may not have analyzed its cause. The cause is very simple: nature allows you to fix your mind on whatever you desire and create your own plan for attaining it; then it places behind your efforts all those benefits that come to you in the sealed envelope labeled, "Riches you may have in return for taking possession of your own mind and directing it to ends of your own choosing."

It is clear why success attracts more success. It is equally clear why failure attracts more failure if you have neglected to take possession of your mind and put it to work. Truly nature discourages idleness and penalizes it wherever it exists.

With a positive mental attitude, you can put your mind to work believing in success and opulence as your right: your belief will guide you unerringly toward whatever your definition of these may be. With that same mind operating through a negative mental attitude, you can believe in fear and frustration, and your mind will attract to you the fruits of these undesirable things.

Now let us break down the contents of these two sealed envelopes and see what they contain. We will call one of these envelopes "Rewards" and the other "Penalties." In the one labeled "Rewards" is a list of some of the blessings it brings:

1. The privilege of placing oneself on the success beam, which attracts only the circumstances which make for success.
2. Sound health, both physically and mentally.
3. Financial independence.
4. A labor of love in which to express oneself.
5. Peace of mind.
6. Applied faith, which makes fear impossible.
7. Enduring friendships.
8. Longevity and a well-balanced life.
9. Immunity against all forms of self-limitation.
10. The wisdom with which to understand oneself and others.

These are some, but not all, of the blessings in that sealed envelope. Now let us examine the envelope labeled "Penalties":

1. Poverty and misery all of one's life.
2. Mental and physical ailments of many kinds.
3. Self-limitation, which binds one to mediocrity all the days of one's life.
4. Fear in all its destructive forms.
5. Dislike of the occupation from which one earns a living.

6. Many enemies, few friends.

7. Every brand of worry known to mankind.

8. Falling victim to every negative influence one encounters.

9. Subjection to the influence and control of other people at their will.

10. A wasted life, which gives nothing to the betterment of mankind.

A positive mental attitude is the most important step we must take in controlling and directing our minds, because a negative mental attitude leaves us wide open to every influence we contact, especially negative ones. A positive mental attitude is the only condition of the mind in which we can gain the wisdom to recognize the true purpose of life and adapt ourselves to that purpose. A positive mental attitude is a must for all who make life pay off in their own terms.

Steps you can take to develop a positive mental attitude:

1. Recognize your privilege of taking possession of and using your own mind as the one and the only thing over which you have complete control.

2. Recognize and prove to your own satisfaction the truth that every adversity carries with it the seed of an equivalent benefit.

3. Close the door behind you on all the failures and unpleasant circumstances you have experienced in the past.

4. Put into action that magic success principle: the habit of going the extra mile.

5. Select a pacemaker and emulate him or her in every possible way.

6. Determine how much material wealth you require, set up a plan for acquiring it, then place a stopgap on your ambitions to be richer by adopting the principle of not too much, not too little. By this you can guide your future ambitions for material things.

7. Form the habit of daily saying or doing something that will make someone else feel better.

8. Convince yourself that ultimately nothing matters as far as you personally are concerned, giving yourself immunity against all petty causes of worry.

9. Find out what you like best to do, discover a labor of love, and do it with all your heart and soul, even if it is only a hobby.

10. Communicate with anyone whom you know you have unjustly offended by word or deed, offer adequate apologies, and ask forgiveness.

11. Remember always that no one can hurt your feelings, make you angry, or frighten you without your full cooperation and consent.

12. Learn the art of mastering your love emotions by exercising them under conditions of your own making through the principle of diversion or transmutation.

13. Discover that self-pity is an insidious destroyer of self-reliance and recognize that the one person on whom you can and should depend at all times is yourself. Remember, as long as anyone can hurt your feelings for any cause or make you angry against your will, there are weak spots in your mental equipment. These need to be mended before you can express yourself through a positive mental attitude.

14. Form the habit of tolerance and keep an open mind on all subjects toward people of all races and creeds.

15. Learn to like people as they are instead of demanding of them to be as you wish them to be. You have to live with people; therefore learn to like them, and eventually you will recognize that love and affection constitute the finest medicine for both your body and your soul. Love changes the entire chemistry of the body and conditions it for expressing a positive mental attitude. Love also extends the space one may occupy in the hearts of one's fellow humans. Important also is the fact that love is free, and the best way to receive it is by giving it.

Now we come to a subject of paramount importance in developing and maintaining a positive mental attitude: believing where belief is justified. You should acquire an enduring belief in the existence of Infinite Intelligence, from which your Creator arranged that you should receive the power to help you take possession of your own mind and direct it to whatever ends you may choose. You should acquire an enduring belief in your own ability to become free and self-determining as your greatest gift from your Creator, and you should demonstrate this belief in actions befitting its nature.

You should believe in those with whom you are associated in connection with your occupation or calling of life. If they are not worthy of your complete belief in them, you have the wrong associates.

Finally, you can believe in the power of the spoken word, and see to it that you speak no word that does not harmonize in every respect with your positive mental attitude.

At this point, I shall present some suggestions of vital importance to those who desire to assimilate this philosophy of success and apply it to achieve the things they desire most in life.

1. Adjust yourself to other people's state of mind and their peculiarities so as to get along peacefully with them. Refrain from taking notice of trivial circum-

stances in human relations, and refuse to allow them to become controversial incidents.

2. Establish your own technique for conditioning your mind at the start of each day so you can maintain a positive mental attitude throughout the day.

3. Adopt the habit of having a healthy laugh as a means of transmuting anger into a harmless emotion. Observe how effectively this will change the entire chemistry of your mind from negative to positive.

4. Concentrate your mind on the can-do portion of all the tasks you undertake. Do not worry about the cannot-do portion unless and until it meets you face-to-face.

5. Learn to look upon life as a continuous process of learning from experiences, both the good and the bad. Be always alert for gains in wisdom, which come a little at a time, day by day, through both pleasant and unpleasant experiences.

6. Remember always that every thought you release comes back greatly multiplied to bless or curse you. Watch your thought releases, and make sure you send out only those thoughts whose fruits you are willing to receive in return.

7. Be careful of your associates, because the negative mental attitude of other people is very contagious, and it rubs off a little at a time.

8. Remember that prayer brings the best results when the one who is praying has sufficient faith to see himself already in possession of that for which he prays. This calls for a positive mental attitude of the highest order.

Peace of mind can be obtained only by a positive mental attitude. And right here we are beginning to recognize that peace of mind, like everything else, has a price one must pay in order to get it and to keep it. The price:

1. Recognition of the truth that the universal power of Infinite Intelligence is available to all who will learn how to use it.

2. The habit of helping others to help themselves.

3. Freedom from all desire for revenge.

4. The habit of going the extra mile in all human relationships.

5. Knowing who you are and knowing your true virtues and abilities which distinguish you from all other people.

6. Freedom from discouragement of every nature.

7. The habit of thinking in terms of what one desires.

8. The habit of starting where one stands in order to do what one has set one's heart upon.

9. The habit of conquering the petty misfortunes of daily occurrences instead of being mastered by them.

10. The habit of looking for the seed of an equivalent benefit in all adversities.

11. The habit of taking life in its stride, neither shrinking from the disagreeable nor overindulging in pleasures.

12. The habit of giving before trying to get.

13. The joy of getting happiness from doing rather than from possessing.

14. The habit of evaluating poverty only as a disease to be conquered and transmuted into desirable assets.

15. Engaging in a labor of love of one's own choice.

These are some of the joys of exercising a positive mental attitude.

Form a mental picture of yourself as a pillar of strength and power, immediately blocking out any negative thoughts. You're ten feet tall, filled with self-confidence. Isn't that a wonderful feeling? Hold that image in your mind, and remember this exhilarating feeling. Now enthusiastically repeat these words:

> ↝ *I am always positive, prosperous-minded, and filled with self-confidence.*

> ↝ *I am always positive, prosperous-minded, and filled with self-confidence.*

> ↝ *I am always positive, prosperous-minded, and filled with self-confidence.*

> ↝ *I am always positive, prosperous-minded, and filled with self-confidence.*

→ *I am always positive, prosperous-minded, and filled with self-confidence.*

→ *I am always positive, prosperous-minded, and filled with self-confidence.*

→ *I am always positive, prosperous-minded, and filled with self-confidence.*

→ *I am always positive, prosperous-minded, and filled with self-confidence.*

→ *I am always positive, prosperous-minded, and filled with self-confidence.*

→ *I am always positive, prosperous-minded, and filled with self-confidence.*

14

Accurate Thinking

We now approach the mystery of all mysteries: the power of the human mind. Let us approach this subject in a spirit of awe, for it is the most profound subject of this entire philosophy. It holds the secret of all successes and all failures. It is the one principle that is, of necessity, on the must list of all who would attain the master key of riches and all who would gain entrance to the great estate of happiness. It is the most important subject known to mankind, yet paradoxically, it is the least understood of all subjects: accurate thinking.

The power of thought may be likened to a rich garden spot whose soil may, by organized effort, be used to produce necessary products of food, or, by its neglect, may be allowed to produce useless weeds. The mind is eternally at work, building up or tearing down, bringing misery, unhappiness, and poverty or joy, pleasure, and riches. It is never idle. It is the greatest of all the assets available to mankind, yet it is the least used and the most abused. Its abuse consists mainly in its nonuse.

Science has revealed many of nature's most profound secrets but not the secret of humanity's greatest source of riches: the power of thought. This is perhaps because mankind has shown such unpardonable indifference toward this divine gift. The power of thought is the most dangerous or the most beneficial power available to man, depending upon how it is used. Through the power of thought, man builds great empires of civilization. Through the same power, other men trample down empires as if they were so much helpless clay. Every human creation, whether good or bad, is created first in a thought pattern. All ideas are conceived through thought. All plans, purposes, and desires are created in thought, and thought is the only thing over which humanity has been given the complete privilege of control.

Let us examine the steps to accurate thinking so that we may direct personal initiative to attain any desired purpose. Accurate thinking is based upon two major fundamentals: (1) inductive reasoning, based on the assumption of unknown facts or hypotheses; (2) deductive reasoning, based on known facts or what are believed to be facts. Accurate thinkers, when dealing with facts, take these important steps as a means of making their thinking effective: (1) they separate facts from fiction or hearsay evidence; (2) they separate facts into classes: important and unimportant.

Most people do not think; they just think that they think. Most so-called thinking is nothing but an expression of feeling through the emotions, and the emotions are not dependable. The accurate thinker always submits his emotional desires and decisions to his head for judiciary examination before he relies upon them as sound, for he knows that his head is more dependable than is his heart. The most commonly expressed emotions, and the more dangerous on that account, are these: (1) fear, (2) love, (3) anger, (4) jealousy, (5) revenge, (6) vanity, (7) greed. These are the seven robber barons that too often rob individuals of their opportunity for achievement by making accurate thinking impossible. They should be under constant control and always subject to the closest scrutiny, for they lead to errors of judgment.

All thought habits come from one or the other of two sources, both of them hereditary. The first is *physical heredity*. From this source, one inherits something of the nature and character of all the generations of the human race that have preceded him. This inheritance is fixed by the laws of nature, but much of it can be modified in preparation for accurate thinking. The second source is *social heredity*, consisting of all environmental influences, education, experience, and impulses of thought produced by external stimuli. The greater portion of all thinking is inspired by social heredity. This is the same as saying that most of our thinking is made to order for us by others.

The accurate thinker recognizes all the facts of life, both the good and the bad, and assumes the responsibility of separating and organizing the two, choosing those that serve his needs and rejecting all the others. He is not impressed by hearsay evidence. He is not the slave but the master of his own emotions. He lives among others without allowing them to encroach upon his inner thoughts or his method of thinking. His opinions are the result of sober analysis and careful study of facts or dependable evidence. He avails himself of the counsel of others but reserves to himself the right to accept or reject it without apologies. When his plans fail, he promptly builds other plans to take their place, but he is never deflected from his purpose by temporary defeat. He is a philosopher, who determines causes by analyzing their effects. He gets most of his cues by observing the laws of nature and adapting himself to them.

When the accurate thinker prays, his first request is for more wisdom, but he never insults the Deity by asking for the circumvention of any natural law or demanding something for nothing. Thus his prayers are usually answered and in full, for he has thrown himself on the side of his Creator. He does not covet the material possessions of others, for he has a better way of acquiring all of his needs—by first earning them. He does not envy others, because he knows that he is richer than most others in the values that count most in life. He gives aid to others freely and accepts it only when its acceptance has been fully justified.

These are the traits of an accurate thinker. Study them carefully if you would become one of the small minority who think accurately. The traits are simple and easily understood, but not so easily cultivated, for cultivation requires more self-discipline than the majority of people are willing to exercise, but the reward for accurate thinking is worthy of the effort to obtain that reward. It consists of many values, among them peace of mind, freedom of body and mind, wisdom, understanding of the laws of nature, the material necessities of life, and above all, harmony with the great scheme of the universe as it is established and maintained by the Creator. No one can deny that the accurate thinker has established a working relationship with his Creator.

Accurate thinking is a priceless asset that cannot be purchased with money or borrowed from others. It must be self-attained through the strictest habits of self-discipline as gathered, organized, and tested through the experiences of successful men and women in many walks of life.

It is the rarest experience to find a person who lives his own life, thinks his own thoughts, develops his own habits, and makes even the slightest attempt to be himself. Most people are imitators of others, and many are neurotics who would rather keep up with the Joneses than be themselves. Observe those you know best. Study their habits carefully, and you will realize that most of them are merely synthetic imitations of other people, without a thought they can truthfully call their own. Most people trail along, accepting and acting upon the thoughts and habits of others, much as sheep trail along after one another over established paths in the pastures. Once in a great while, some individual with a tendency toward accurate thinking will pull away from the crowd, think his own thoughts, and dare to be himself. When you find such a person, behold, you are face-to-face with a thinker.

Let us now observe what these two important principles, habit and social heredity, reveal. The law that forces upon every living creature the dominance of the environment in which it lives is a natural law that cannot be modified, changed, or circumvented. It is called *social heredity*, but it can be used to great advantage by combining with it the principle of controlled habit (and let us remember that all voluntary habits can be controlled).

Here, then, begins the story of organized thinking, which we wish to present in terms so simple that any child may understand them. Think deeply, for we are approaching one of the greatest of all miracles—the power of creative thought, through which one may translate thought impulses into their physical, financial, or spiritual equivalents. If there is one portion of this philosophy that is more profound than any other, it is this one, for we are dealing with the real source of the power behind all human achievements—the power that is responsible, through its misuse because of our ignorance, for much of the misery of mankind, the power that brings success or failure according to the way it is applied.

Let us convey the picture through a familiar comparison. Let us assume that we are taking a physical picture of the power of thought, using the mind as the sensitive plate of the camera and controlled habit as the lens through which any desired object may be photographed. The plate of the camera will register any object reflected upon it by light projected through the lens. It does not pick and choose but registers everything that is cast upon it. To make a clear picture, the lens must be properly focused, and the object to be photographed must be flooded with the proper amount of light. All of this depends upon the skill and accuracy of the one who is operating the camera. Thus the operator works through controlled habit.

Now let us shift the scene from the camera to the human brain so that we may observe how perfectly the two resemble each other in their operation. The individual chooses the subject he wishes to register in the cells of his brain, the brain serving as the sensitized plate of the camera. He calls the subject a *definite major purpose*. He desires the brain to pick up a clear picture of that purpose in all of its detail in order to register it and convey it to the subconscious for translation into its physical equivalent by whatever natural means may be available. Therefore he proceeds, through the principle of controlled habit, to place in his conscious mind a clear picture of what he desires. Day after day he repeats that picture through controlled habit, because he recognizes, as the accurate thinker always does, that the mental impulse of thought through which he is painting the picture in his brain must be given the right amount of time, through repeated exposures, to register properly. It must also be accompanied by the proper proportion of light—emotional feeling mixed with reason— to enable the brain to pick up a clear outline and all the details of the thought.

In conveying to the brain a clear picture of what one desires to have translated into its physical equivalent, one must take four important steps, all of which are easily followed and are subject to individual control. They are: (1) adoption of a definite major purpose; (2) the creation of a practical plan for the attainment of that purpose; (3) a Master Mind alliance with others whose experience, skill, or influence may be needed for the purpose; (4) immediate and continuous action in carrying out the plan.

Thought must be well supported with emotional feeling, the most powerful of which is the emotion of faith. The necessary support may be given to thought by the application of eight principles of this philosophy:

1. **Definiteness of purpose**. Begin with this principle by adopting an objective based on a definite motive or desire for its attainment.

2. **The Master Mind**. Through this principle, one should ally himself with others with the necessary education, skill, and experience to aid him in the attainment of his definite purpose.

3. **Personal initiative**. One must apply this principle by taking the initiative and carrying out his plans for attaining his purpose.

4. **Creative vision**. One must use this principle, through the faculty of the imagination, as an aid in choosing Master Mind allies and building ingenious plans for attaining one's purpose.

5. **Self-discipline**. This principle must be applied to ensure that every faculty of the mind will be organized and directed toward the attainment of one's major purpose and to prevent quitting when the going becomes difficult.

6. **Applied faith**. This principle must be applied to provide the individual with the necessary hope and self-

reliance to ensure continuous action in the pursuit of his plans and to give him contact with Infinite Intelligence for the wisdom he needs.

7. **A pleasing personality.** This principle must be applied as a means of influencing others to cooperate and to sell the individual's ideas or plans to other people with a minimum amount of resistance.

8. **The habit of going the extra mile**. This principle should be applied as a means of creating friendly allies and earning the right to ask for the cooperation of others, thus placing them in a position where they will desire to cooperate.

The combined application of these eight principles, when supported by accurate thinking, constitutes organized thought in the highest order known to mankind. How could anyone be permanently defeated who has acquired the ability to transmute every emotion, every feeling, every fear, and every worry into a positive driving force for attaining definite ends? This is precisely what organized thinking enables one to do: it organizes all the faculties of the mind and conditions them for the expression of faith. "Thoughts are things," said the great philosopher, and again, thought is the only power over which any individual has been provided by the Creator with complete control.

As a seeker of truth, picture yourself as always capable of recognizing facts, both good and bad. You are not impressed by hearsay evidence, and you are master of your own emotions, able to organize your thoughts to the positive attainment of your goal. Think and repeat several times a day:

↝ *I am able to organize my thoughts and emotions into a positive driving force toward my goal.*

↝ *I am able to organize my thoughts and emotions into a positive driving force toward my goal.*

↝ *I am able to organize my thoughts and emotions into a positive driving force toward my goal.*

↝ *I am able to organize my thoughts and emotions into a positive driving force toward my goal.*

↝ *I am able to organize my thoughts and emotions into a positive driving force toward my goal.*

↝ *I am able to organize my thoughts and emotions into a positive driving force toward my goal.*

↝ *I am able to organize my thoughts and emotions into a positive driving force toward my goal.*

↝ *I am able to organize my thoughts and emotions into a positive driving force toward my goal.*

↝ *I am able to organize my thoughts and emotions into a positive driving force toward my goal.*

↝ *I am able to organize my thoughts and emotions into a positive driving force toward my goal.*

↝ *I am able to organize my thoughts and emotions into a positive driving force toward my goal.*

15

Sound Physical Health

This chapter is not a treatise on disease or the treatment of diseases. Its purpose is to alert your mind to a sound health consciousness. You see, the physical body is a temple provided by the Creator to serve as a dwelling place for the mind. It is the most perfect mechanism ever produced, and it is practically self-maintaining. It has a brain, which serves as a center of the nervous system and the coordinator of all bodily activity, the receiver of all sense perceptions, and the organ which, by means as yet unexplained by science, coordinates all perceptions, knowledge, and memory into new patterns, which we know as thought.

The mind and the body are so closely related that whatever the one does affects the other. The brain is the commander of all voluntary movements of the body as well as of all involuntary movements carried on through the subconscious, such as breathing, the heartbeat, digestion, circulation of the blood, distribution of nervous energy, and the like. It is the storehouse of all knowledge, the interpreter of the influences of environment and thought. It is the most powerful and the least understood organ of the body. The brain is the housing of the subconscious as well as the conscious mind, but the energy and the intelligence that produce thought flow into the brain from the great universal storehouse of Infinite Intelligence; the brain serves only as a receiver and distributor of this energy.

The mind and body relationship has much to do with health. The brain operates a first-class department of chemistry through which it breaks up and assimilates the food taken into the stomach, liquifies the food, and distributes it through the bloodstream to every part of the body, where it is needed for maintenance and repair of the individual cells. All of this service is performed automatically, but the individual can give certain simple aids to the brain that will help maintain sound physical health. In addition, many physical ailments are caused or aggravated by mental and emotional upsets. Many of such ailments can be prevented by mental and emotional self-control. This chapter should serve as a practical program, helpful to those having the courage, determination, and self-control to follow it.

Sound health begins with a sound health consciousness, just as financial success begins with a prosperity consciousness. No one ever succeeds financially without prosperity consciousness, nor does one enjoy sound physical health without health consciousness. Ponder this statement thoughtfully, for it conveys a truth that is of paramount benefit for sound physical health. To maintain a health consciousness, one must think in terms of sound health, not in terms of illness and disease. In one sentence, the French psychologist Émile Coué gave the world a simple but practical formula for the maintenance of a health consciousness: *Day by day, in every way, I am getting better and better.* He recommended repeating this sentence thousands of times daily until the subconscious section of the mind picks it up, accepts it, and begins to carry it out to its logical conclusion in the form of good health. Many people have accepted the Coué formula in good faith, put it to work in earnest, and discovered that it produced marvelous results, for it started them on the road toward health consciousness.

Banish worry and fear by maintaining your positive mental attitude. If you are to maintain a health consciousness, fear and worry should have no place in your life, for they will surely undermine good health. Learn the habit of emotional control. Such emotions as malice, revenge, and resentment produce toxins, poisons in the blood. Maintain a positive mental attitude at all times, for this will produce a healthful influence. All thought energy, whether it is positive or negative, is carried to every cell of the body and there deposited as energy by which the cells operate. The energy of thought is carried to the cells of the body through the nervous system and the bloodstream, because the chemist of the body mixes the energy of thought with every particle of food that is assimilated and projected into the bloodstream.

From a rational viewpoint, most ailments are the result of disobeying the laws of nature, for which we must pay in pain and suffering. Pains have a purpose: to warn you that you need to change your habit of living. Once we learn to partake of all good things in moderation, we have learned the most important secret of healthful living. It will assure us of enjoying life to its fullest.

Corrective posture: Good posture is more than fine figure. It advertises the well-being of the entire personality and indicates a complete and balanced activity. The right position of the body is a vital issue to all who really desire good health. Good posture contributes to good health, poor posture to poor health. This idea is based on the mechanics of the human body. Good posture means that the framework of the body is in the position intended by nature, enabling the bodily organs to function in their normal position; it means that nerves and blood vessels are in the best condition to keep the organs strong and healthy.

Foods for fitness: Our body is made up of what we eat. When we furnish it with the needed requirements for growth and repair, we add length to our life, along with health, strength, and the joy of living. Our first food is air, our second water, and our third the living elements in food, which we classify as vitamins and minerals.

Air: To breathe properly, the body must be erect, whether in a standing, walking, or sitting posture. If the body is allowed to slump, the lungs are cramped so that they cannot fully expand, and the muscles that control breathing are hampered in their movements. Breathing from waistline to neckline includes the whole of the lungs from top to bottom—practice deep breathing until it becomes a habit. Learn to inhale and exhale completely.

Water: Next to the air we breathe, water is the most important foodstuff in our lives. It makes up about half the volume of our blood and is used to carry the food elements to every living cell. If the body is unable to get enough water, unhealthy conditions result. It would be well to drink a glass of water upon awakening each morning, one glass with each meal, and one or two glasses of water between meals.

Vitamins and minerals: Food serves the body in three distinct ways: (1) by supplying fuel for body energy; (2) by providing material for the building and upkeep of body organs and tissues; (3) by furnishing protective materials. Vitamins and minerals, which regulate body functions, aid the body in utilizing other foods and enable it to manufacture substances of its own. A diet of a wide variety of fruits, fresh vegetables, whole grain cereals, and milk, with moderate quantities of seafood and meats, will supply the body's mineral needs. These same foods, incidentally, are good sources of vitamins; therefore they do double duty in keeping the body in a good state of nutrition. Check with your doctor to see that your diet has adequate mineral and vitamin content.

Eating habits: We can all help ourselves to improve digestion by following these suggestions: (1) Food should be chewed thoroughly before it is swallowed. (2) For best digestion, food should be tasty. (3) Food should be eaten in moderate amounts. (4) Do not do heavy physical work immediately after a meal. (5) Eat a balanced ration, consisting of at least a fair proportion of fruits and vegetables. (6) The mind must be conditioned and prepared for eating. One should never eat while angry, frightened, or worried. Conversation while eating should be of a pleasant nature and never too intense. Family disagreements and discipline should never take place during mealtime. The mealtime should be a time when all negative states of mind have been discarded. It should be an expression of gratitude to the Creator for having prepared so great an abundance of necessities of life for every living creature, not an hour for ugly expressions and negative thinking.

Relaxation: Relaxation means the complete letting go of both the body and the mind, particularly clearing the mind of all worries, fears, and anxieties. There should be a period of not less than one hour in each day during which the body and the mind are habitually relaxed and released from all voluntary effort. Learn to relax even while you work. Let your muscles be as loose as possible. You will do your job more easily and save wear and tear on your nervous system. If you can lie down and rest during the day, even for as short a period as thirty minutes, you will lengthen the span of your life. Avoid fatigue; it is a killer. Fatigue produces poisons that injure the nervous system and hasten the onset of old age. When you are tired, rest promptly and completely. To drive yourself to the point of exhaustion is to court disaster.

Restful sleep: Sleep is one of the most important functions of life. Shakespeare called sleep "sore labour's bath" and "chief nourisher in life's feast." Doctors are frequently asked how much sleep should a person have. Dr. L. J. Steinbach of Pittsburgh, Pennsylvania, nationally known scientist, has written an excellent paper on this subject, from which we quote in part:

Requirements According to Age. The 8 out of 24-hour rule for sleep applies best to adults between the ages of 21 and 50. While it is popularly accepted that older persons sleep less, this does not mean that they need less rest. After 50, the physical body should have 10 hours or more divided between sleep and rest. After 60, not less than twelve hours out of 24. Mental activity is not so exhausting in later years of life as physical activity. In childhood and adolescence, the sleeping period should be from 10 to twelve hours.

The growing tendency to shorten the length of rest in order to meet many new demands upon our time is regarded by nearly all researchers as an insidious danger to health.

When you hang up your clothes and prepare for bed, hang up also all worries, problems, fears, and anxieties, leaving your mind free to concentrate upon this relaxation for restful sleep procedure: Lie on your back, hands alongside your body. Stretch tall and then relax. Do this a few times, and then you are ready to put the different parts of your body to sleep.

Avoid the habit of self-prescribed drugs. Nature provided humanity with a very good supply of medicine for the maintenance of sound health, but she stores it in vegetables and fruits in the natural state in the form of minerals. All of these minerals can be taken in the form of prepared pills and liquid medicines, but they appear to serve nature's purpose much better if they are taken in their natural form, from food that grows from the soil.

Moreover, Infinite Intelligence has provided every person with an expert chemist who understands the exact proportion of each of these minerals that is needed for the maintenance of sound health. When a cure is effected normally, it is nature that does the curing; in most cases, doctors merely cooperate with nature in treating disease. Painkillers never cure disease. When you administer them to yourself, you are tearing down nature's warning signal with but temporary relief. Find out how your body functions. Study the combinations of food required by your particular system and working habits. Acquire moderation in your eating habits. Use self-discipline in all your habits. Thus you will express your highest form of gratitude toward your Creator.

The habit of fasting: Weight correction is not the only function of fasting, for every animal that is lower in the scale of intelligence than man resorts to fasting for practically every physical ill. Fasting gives a needed rest to both the body and the mind. It gives the stomach and other vital organs, including the heart and the kidneys, time to catch up with their back work and the overwork that have been forced upon them by intemperate habits. Short fasts of from one to three days should be taken from time to time whenever one feels dull and sluggish and lacking in vitality. Sometimes a single day's fast will work wonders in a person's physical condition.

Look to your health and, if you have it, praise God and value it next to a good conscience, for health is the second blessing that we mortals are capable of, a blessing that money cannot buy. Imagine yourself as perfectly healthy and sound in mind and body, with a keen awareness of all that is good for you, such as proper food, rest, relaxation, a consciousness of perfect health. Now repeat these words:

→ *I am perfectly healthy, mentally and physically, and I do all things to properly maintain my health.*

→ *I am perfectly healthy, mentally and physically, and I do all things to properly maintain my health.*

→ *I am perfectly healthy, mentally and physically, and I do all things to properly maintain my health.*

→ *I am perfectly healthy, mentally and physically, and I do all things to properly maintain my health.*

→ *I am perfectly healthy, mentally and physically, and I do all things to properly maintain my health.*

→ *I am perfectly healthy, mentally and physically, and I do all things to properly maintain my health.*

→ *I am perfectly healthy, mentally and physically, and I do all things to properly maintain my health.*

→ *I am perfectly healthy, mentally and physically, and I do all things to properly maintain my health.*

→ *I am perfectly healthy, mentally and physically, and I do all things to properly maintain my health.*

→ *I am perfectly healthy, mentally and physically, and I do all things to properly maintain my health.*

16

Cooperation

Cooperation, like love and friendship, is something one may get by giving. The road that leads to happiness has many fellow travelers on it. You will need their cooperation, and they will need yours. The teamwork we engage in today may make this country more livable for our children and for the children of other men, who have a right to expect something from us besides a mountain of public debts. Remember, you appropriate this philosophy from the men who provided it. Remember that you owe something to those who will follow you. This nation must go on. The American standard of living must be maintained and raised even higher. Our system of free enterprise must be preserved. Our form of democracy must be protected. Our schools and churches must be given a firm foundation, and our sources of financial income must be made secure for the benefit of those who will follow us, just as they have been preserved for us by those who have preceded us.

Let us now turn our attention to the methods by which successful men have profited by understanding and applying the principle of teamwork. We live in a material world, and one of our major responsibilities is to gain economic security while serving as bridge builders for others. Teamwork and a spirit of friendliness cost little in the way of time and effort and pay huge dividends, not only in money but in the finer things of life. This spirit lights the path to happiness for all who adopt it, and it is the spirit that leads to the attainment of the twelve riches of life: (1) a positive mental attitude; (2) sound physical health; (3) harmony in human relationships; (4) freedom from fear; (5) hope of achievement; (6) the capacity for faith: (7) a willingness to share one's blessings; (8) a labor of love; (9) an open mind on all subjects; (10) self-discipline; (11) the capacity to understand people; and (12) economic security. What an array of riches! And each of them is tied in with that little word *teamwork*. Each and every one of these great riches is directly related to the principle of cooperation. Learn to cooperate in a spirit of friendliness, and you will be well on the way to acquiring all of these riches.

Edwin C. Barnes was proud of his association with the great Edison. Several years after he began with Edison, he was telling of his experiences and mentioned that his business association with the inventor was yielding him an income of $12,000 a year.

"What?" exclaimed his friend. "You're a partner of the great Edison but are making only $12,000 a year? Why, if I had your opportunity, I would be earning ten times that amount."

That was not exactly the reaction Mr. Barnes had expected, but he managed to pull himself together and asked how.

"How? I'll tell you how," the friend replied. "You are engaged in selling the Edison dictating machine, called the Ediphone, and you naturally have a force of salesmen in the field. If I were in your place, I would form a friendly, cooperative working arrangement between my salesmen and the salesmen of other concerns who are selling related merchandise. Dictating machines are sold to businessmen who also use typewriters, desks, filing cabinets, printing and adding machines, cash registers, office supplies, and general office equipment. Therefore I would form an alliance between my sales organization and the salesmen in each of these fields, through which there would be an exchange of favors. I would instruct my salesmen to keep their eyes open for opportunities to sell these general office products and to turn into my office the names of all prospective buyers of such merchandise. Then I would turn these names over to the salesmen of the various office supplies in return for a similar service from them. In other words, the salesmen of office supplies would supply my salesmen with the names of firms that might need Edison dictating machines, and my salesmen would supply them with the names of firms that might need office equipment. This teamwork would cost no one anything except the time necessary to write down the names on cards and hand them in, but it would provide both groups of salesmen with all the sales leads they could handle. Now do you get the idea, my friend?"

"Yes," Barnes replied, "I think I do."

The results were immediate and encouraging. Mr. Barnes' income began to rise by leaps and bounds until it reached far beyond a ten times increase over his $12,000 a year income. There are no patent rights on Mr. Barnes' plan of friendly cooperation, and it requires no great amount of skill or experience to adapt the plan to one's own need. It is a well-known fact that all successes in the higher brackets of achievement are due to teamwork.

Andrew Carnegie stated numberless times that his huge fortune was accumulated through the teamwork of other men who were associated with him in his Master Mind alliance. His alliance with Charles M. Schwab was a notable example of how two men may benefit by working together toward a definite end. Mr. Carnegie lifted Mr. Schwab from the lowly position of a day laborer and gave him an opportunity to become a great industrial leader, with its attendant financial compensations. On the other hand, Mr. Schwab became Mr. Carnegie's right-hand man and helped him to build a great industrial empire, which benefited millions of men and women, whom, directly and indirectly, it provided with employment.

Wherever the spirit of teamwork is the dominating influence in business or industry, success is inevitable. We take you now to Baltimore, Maryland, where we shall look in on the business operations of McCormick and Company, manufacturers and importers of teas and spices. The plan under which management and workers are related in the business is known as the "multiple management plan," which is another way of describing the company's policy of teamwork. Before I describe the multiple management plan, let us take notice of some of the benefits of the plan, which provides every employee with a definite motive for doing his best under all circumstances, thus ensuring each employee the opportunity to promote himself on his own merits to whatever position he may be qualified to fill.

First of all, the multiple management plan inspires every individual connected with the company with a definite major purpose: a deep-seated desire to contribute to the company's success. It develops self-reliance through self-expression that is free from all fears. It encourages the spirit of clean sportsmanship inside and outside of the business. It develops leadership by encouraging the exercise of personal initiative and a willingness to assume personal responsibility. It inspires teamwork between employees and the management, eliminating the usual tendency of people to pass the buck and dodge individual responsibility. It develops alertness of the mind and keenness of the imagination. It provides an adequate outlet for the expression of individual ambition on a basis that is highly beneficial to each individual associated with the company. It gives everyone a feeling of belonging, and no one is left without the means of gaining personal recognition on merit. It inspires loyalty among the employees, loyalty to the company, and to one another; thus labor troubles are unknown. It gives the company the fullest possible benefit of all talents, ingenuity, and creative vision of every employee and provides adequate compensation for these talents in proportion to their value.

Now let us examine the plan as it has been described by Robert Little in *Reader's Digest*:

Something that an ambitious and capable young friend of mine said the other day seemed to me a significant criticism of the way too many American businesses are run, all the more significant because it echoed complaints we've all heard time and again or perhaps personally felt. "I have something to give to our company which it does not seem to want," said my friend. "The management is somewhere way up in the clouds and I have no contact with it. At first I tried making suggestions but soon learned to keep my mouth shut and do as I was told. In frequent speeches to us, the employees, the president, who hardly recognizes me when he sees me in the elevator, asks me to be loyal as if loyalty were a one-way street. The few raises I've gotten I've had to beg for and they were granted grudgingly, but more than money, I want recognition, freedom, a sense of being really in on the company's affairs. The aloofness of the higher-ups makes a lot of us juniors fall into a I-don't-care attitude. I think it does the firm more harm than a sit-down strike."

Such a complaint could not be made by the employees of McCormick and Company, for the company, through its multiple management plan, has found out a way to draw upon hidden resources of energy, initiative, and enthusiasm often neglected by centralized management and has learned how to enlist the hearts as well as the heads of men who work for it. For 43 years, this spice, tea, and extract business was run by the founder, Willoughby M. McCormick, a genius. Upon his death in 1932, he was succeeded by his nephew, Charles P. McCormick. Young McCormick, even after 17 years of apprenticeship, did not feel able to assume a one-man crown. He wanted to share responsibilities with those who could be taught to take it. He felt that independence must be restored to an organization sunk in routine and that creative imagination should be revived among men who had been saying "yes" to one man's mind so long that they were using only half of their own. The company's board of directors were men of 45 and over. Their habits of thought were colored by the past; something more was needed. And so, out of necessity was born the idea of multiple management.

McCormick picked 17 younger men from various departments and said to them, "You are the junior board of directors. You will supplement the senior board and feed it with ideas. Elect your own chairman and secretary. Discuss everything that concerns the business. The books are open to you, and the minds of your superiors will be wide open to you also. Make any recommendation you like on one condition: it must be unanimous."

I saw the junior board in action—17 young men around a long table, each one bursting with ideas for raising the business a notch higher. The atmosphere was free. There was plenty of kidding but over it all was the shadow of that day, twice a year, when the junior board elects three new members after dropping the three whom a ballot declares to have been the least efficient.

At this point, some businessmen may inquire, "All very pretty and democratic, but does it pay?" Yes, it pays. The company overhead is 12% under 1929. Labor turnover is down to 6% a year, to less than that for the younger employees. It pays the rank and file employees with bonuses at Christmas, larger every year for the last five years, and a minimum wage double that of the prosperity peak and way above the wage for similar work in Baltimore. The total payroll is 34% higher than it was in 1929, but production is just 34% higher also. Although the organization consists of around 2,000 employees, every employee's individuality is so scrupulously protected and preserved that he has as good an opportunity to attract attention to himself as he would have if the organization were small. Thus the McCormick multiple management plan has at least eliminated one of the major curses of large industrial organizations where too often men lose their individual identity in the crowd and only the bold and aggressive have an opportunity to promote themselves by attracting attention to their work. As almost everyone knows, most men will work harder for personal recognition and a word of commendation where it is deserved than they will for money alone. Through the multiple management plan, McCormick and Company has put the soul back into its industry. It has provided every worker with a multiple motive to go the extra mile and to do it in the right sort of mental attitude.

Teamwork differs from the Master Mind principle in that it is based on the coordination of effort without necessarily embracing the principle of definiteness of purpose or the principle of harmony, two important essentials of the Master Mind. There are two types of teamwork: (1) willing teamwork, based upon voluntary coordination of effort and free from all forms of force; (2) unwilling teamwork, based upon fear, force, or some necessity. The difference between these types determines whether any form of cooperation shall be permanent and constructive or temporary and destructive.

Willing teamwork is the only type that leads to constructive ends, that ensures permanency of power through the coordination of effort. Men often are forced to cooperate in carrying out a given plan or purpose, sometimes by economic necessity, sometimes by fear, but they do not continue their cooperative effort any longer than the time required for them to eliminate the motive that impelled it. Teamwork produces power, but whether the power is temporary or permanent depends upon the motive that inspired the cooperation. If the motive inspires people to cooperate willingly, the power produced by this sort of teamwork will endure as long as that spirit of willingness prevails. If the motive is one that forces people to cooperate, be it fear or any other negative cause, the power produced will be temporary. Great physical power can be produced by coordination of the efforts of individuals, but the endurance of that power, its quality, scope, and strength, are derived from that intangible something known as the spirit, in which men work together for the attainment of a common end. Where the spirit of teamwork is willing, voluntary, and free, it leads to the attainment of a power that is great and enduring.

Picture yourself a highly enthusiastic team, high in spirits, faith, and confidence, all working in perfect harmony toward a common goal. Truly this is an unbeatable combination. Now say:

→ *I willingly and gladly cooperate with my fellow man in worthwhile teamwork.*

→ *I willingly and gladly cooperate with my fellow man in worthwhile teamwork.*

→ *I willingly and gladly cooperate with my fellow man in worthwhile teamwork.*

→ *I willingly and gladly cooperate with my fellow man in worthwhile teamwork.*

→ *I willingly and gladly cooperate with my fellow man in worthwhile teamwork.*

→ *I willingly and gladly cooperate with my fellow man in worthwhile teamwork.*

→ *I willingly and gladly cooperate with my fellow man in worthwhile teamwork.*

→ *I willingly and gladly cooperate with my fellow man in worthwhile teamwork.*

→ *I willingly and gladly cooperate with my fellow man in worthwhile teamwork.*

→ *I willingly and gladly cooperate with my fellow man in worthwhile teamwork.*

17

Cosmic Habit Force

The purpose of this chapter is to describe and explain the law by which you acquire habits, a law so stupendous in its scope and power that it may be difficult at first to understand. This law is known as *cosmic habit force*, from which you can see that it pertains to the universe as a whole and the laws that govern it.

This law maintains the equilibrium of the whole universe in orderliness through established habits. The law forces every living thing and every inert particle of matter to adhere to and follow the vibrations of its environment, including, of course, the physical habits and the thought habits of mankind. This law forces upon every living creature the dominating influence of its environment. Nature and the universe are organized and ordered. There is order everywhere. The same law that holds our little earth in space and relates it to all the other planets relates human beings to one another in exact conformity with the nature of their own thoughts.

Cosmic habit force is the controller of all natural laws. It is the great law into which all other natural laws resolve. Cosmic habit force is Infinite Intelligence in operation. The thought habits of individuals are automatically fixed and made permanent by cosmic habit force, no matter whether they are negative or positive.

The same force that maintains the precise balance between all the actions and reactions of matter and the time and space relationships of the elements of creation also builds human thought habits with varying degrees of permanency. Negative thought habits of any kind attract to their creator physical manifestations corresponding to their nature, as perfectly and inevitably as nature germinates the acorn and develops it into an oak tree. Through the operation of the same law, positive thoughts reach out into the vast ocean of potential power surrounding us and attract the physical counterparts of their nature.

You create patterns of thought by repeating certain ideas or behavior; the law of cosmic habit force takes over those patterns and makes them more or less permanent unless or until you consciously rearrange them. The method employed by cosmic habit force in converting a positive emotion or desire created in the human mind into its physical equivalent is this: it intensifies that emotion or desire until it induces faith, whereby the mind is receptive to inflowing Infinite Intelligence, whence are derived perfect plans to be followed by the individual for attaining the desired objective. Natural means are used to carry out such plans.

Often a person is awed by what appear to be coincidental combinations of favorable circumstances as he carries out his plans, but these strange and unexplained things happen in a perfectly natural way. Cosmic habit force has the capacity to impart the power to one's thought to surmount all difficulties, remove all obstacles, overcome all resistances. Just what this power is is a secret as profound as the secret that causes a seed of wheat to germinate, grow, and reproduce itself.

We can liken the brain of man to a great river that has a division down its middle. The river is constantly flowing, but one side of it is flowing in one direction, carrying everything that idly drifts into it to certain disappointment and failure. The other half is flowing in the opposite direction and carries onward to success and power everyone who deliberately wades into it. The flowing force of the river of the brain is the power of thought. The failure side of the stream is negative thought; the success side is positive thought. If your life is not what you want it to be, you have let the power of cosmic habit force carry you on the failure side of the river of thought.

Now let's see how cosmic habit force may be of benefit to you in connection with your physical health.

Thinking. A positive mind leads to the development of a health consciousness. Cosmic habit force carries out that thought pattern to its logical conclusion, but it will just as readily carry out the picture of ill-health consciousness created by the thoughts of the hypochondriac, even to the extent of producing the physical and mental symptoms of any disease on which the individual may fix his thoughts through fear.

Eating. The power of one's thoughts enters into and becomes a vital part of the energy that is carried into the body through the food. Worry, fear, and negative thoughts poison the food; therefore controlled thought habits during mealtime are of the utmost importance for maintaining health.

Work. Cosmic habit force may also be connected with your work, the activity to which you devote most of your time and which is the source of your income. Here too your mental attitude becomes a vital ally of the silent repairman who is working on every cell of your body while you are engaged in physical action. Work should be mixed with positive thoughts only.

Elimination of body waste. This process takes place through (1) the liver, (2) the lungs, (3) the pores of the skin, and (4) the alimentary canal. These eliminative processes function rhythmically and in perfect order when supported by the proper thought and diet habits, both patterns being taken over and made permanent by cosmic habit force.

Now we come to the relationship of cosmic habit force to economic and financial benefits—a definite major purpose. This, as you know, is the starting point of all success. You may condition your mind and body to hand over to cosmic habit force the exact pictures through your thought habits of the financial status you wish to maintain; these will be automatically picked up and carried out to their logical conclusion by an unfailing law of nature, which knows no such reality as failure.

Let me call your attention to the proper method of breaking the hold of cosmic habit force on a poverty consciousness and substituting in its place a prosperity consciousness. I have eight princes—imaginary titles I have created in my mind in order to give specific instructions to my subconscious mind (which is where these little folks live). They are (1) the prince of financial prosperity, (2) the prince of sound physical health, (3) the prince of peace of mind, (4) the prince of hope, (5) the prince of faith, (6) the prince of love, (7) the prince of romance, and (8) the prince of overall wisdom. As a part of my daily meditation, I have a conversation with each of these helpful servants, expressing my gratitude to them for the splendid service they render and suggesting ways in which they may be of even greater service.

This technique is very effective for conditioning my mind and balancing the circumstances of my life. These servants of mine are busy forming patterns for cosmic habit force to take over and carry out.

Now here are instructions for you who want to adopt and carry out a definite major purpose in life.

1. Write out a complete, clear, and definite statement of your major purpose in life, sign it, and commit it to memory. Then repeat it orally at least once every day and more often if practicable.

2. Write out a clear, definite plan by which you intend to begin to attain the object of your definite major purpose. State the maximum time allowed for that purpose and precisely what service you are willing to give in return for its realization.

3. Make your plan flexible enough to permit changes at any time you are inspired to do so.

4. Keep your major purpose and your plans for attaining it strictly to yourself except in connection with your Master Mind association.

Now I'm going to give you two types of habits that, if allowed to dwell in your mind, will become fixations and will be carried out until an adversity or accident breaks their grip on you or you deliberately break them through your willpower. Here is the list of negatives: poverty, imaginary illness, laziness, envy, greed, vanity, cynicism, drifting without aim or purpose, irritability, the will to injure others, jealousy, dishonesty, arrogance, and sadism. Here come the positives, and I want you to deliberately start making these fixations in your mind: definiteness of purpose, faith, personal initiative, enthusiasm, willingness to go the extra mile.

I wish to review the means of developing your ego, which will enable you to take advantage of this great law of cosmic habit force by consciously setting up habits for it to embrace.

1. Actively ally yourself with one or more persons who can help you to attain your major purpose.

2. Formulate a plan. Members of your alliance may help you here.

3. Avoid persons and circumstances that make you feel inferior.

4. Close the door on past unpleasant experiences.

5. Surround yourself with the physical means to impress your mind with the nature of your purpose in life.

6. Build your ego with balance, neither over- nor under-inflating it.

Now I want to call your attention to two great forces that, as I have mentioned, are working in the minds of all of us to make us what we are: *social heredity* and *physical heredity*. Physical heredity is the law of nature through which the sum and substance of all the characteristics, traits, and physical aspects of your ancestors back down through the ages have been handed on to you. Social heredity consists of every influence that you will contact from the time you reach a state of consciousness until you die. It's a great day in your life when you break away from your social heredity and start doing your own thinking.

Both social and physical heredity are under the direction of cosmic habit force. Although you are very limited in respect to changing your physical heredity, you can break the grip of cosmic habit force in the case of your social heredity.

There are only three principles underlying the voluntary establishment of a habit, an outcome of your social heredity. They are very important, so remember them well.

1. Plasticity, which simply means the power, property, or capability of changing or being changed.

2. Frequency of impression. One factor affecting the speed with which a habit may be established is how often the impression is made.

3. Intensity of impression. If an idea is impressed upon the mind backed with all the emotion you are capable of—obsessional desire—it will have a greater impact than if you simply express an idle wish, even though the words employed are identical.

The nucleus of this entire philosophy of personal achievement lies in cosmic habit force. All the previous principles lead to the establishment of a positive mental attitude, which puts one in the way to benefit by this master of all natural laws. Control your mental attitude, keeping it positive by exercising self-discipline, thereby preparing the mental soil in which any plan, purpose, or desire may be planted by repeated, intense impression, with the assurance that it will germinate, grow, and ultimately find expression in its material equivalent through whatever means are at hand.

You should now understand the importance of maintaining a positive mental attitude in order to establish patterns of health consciousness and success consciousness. Make mealtime a happy, cheerful event with an attitude of thanksgiving and worship. Approach your work in the same attitude. Balance the four factors of work and play, love and worship in your life. Carefully follow the formula given for building your ego constructively. Deliberately start acquiring habits of thought and action that you need to achieve your purpose in life. If you want to climb out of the rut you are in, you have the means at your disposal for doing so. Change your thought habits.

I sincerely hope that you have enjoyed reading this book of lectures as much as I have enjoyed preparing it. I am going to close these lessons with a saying and a wish borrowed from one of my old favorite radio programs: *I wish for you peace this day and always.*

Now repeat several times daily:

→ *I control my thoughts at all times. I have an alert positive mental attitude, and I persistently think and act in the direction of my good and my goals.*

→ *I control my thoughts at all times. I have an alert positive mental attitude, and I persistently think and act in the direction of my good and my goals.*

→ *I control my thoughts at all times. I have an alert positive mental attitude, and I persistently think and act in the direction of my good and my goals.*

→ *I control my thoughts at all times. I have an alert positive mental attitude, and I persistently think and act in the direction of my good and my goals.*

→ *I control my thoughts at all times. I have an alert positive mental attitude, and I persistently think and act in the direction of my good and my goals.*

→ *I control my thoughts at all times. I have an alert positive mental attitude, and I persistently think and act in the direction of my good and my goals.*

→ *I control my thoughts at all times. I have an alert positive mental attitude, and I persistently think and act in the direction of my good and my goals.*

→ *I control my thoughts at all times. I have an alert positive mental attitude, and I persistently think and act in the direction of my good and my goals.*

→ *I control my thoughts at all times. I have an alert positive mental attitude, and I persistently think and act in the direction of my good and my goals.*

→ *I control my thoughts at all times. I have an alert positive mental attitude, and I persistently think and act in the direction of my good and my goals.*